SEX WARS
Free Adaptations of Ibsen and Strindberg

By the same author

The Method as Means

Theatre at Work (ed.)

The Encore Reader (ed.)

The Tragical History of Doctor Faustus

Confessions of a Counterfeit Critic

Open Space Plays: *An Othello* and *Palach*
(In collaboration with Alan Burns)

The Act of Being

Artaud at Rodez

The Marowitz Shakespeare: *Hamlet, A Macbeth,
The Taming of the Shrew, Measure for Measure,* and
The Merchant of Venice

SEX WARS
Free Adaptations of Ibsen and Strindberg

Hedda
Enemy of the People
The Father

by
CHARLES MAROWITZ

Marion Boyars
Boston . London

Published in The United States and Great Britain in 1982 by
MARION BOYARS Inc.,
99 Main Street,
Salem, New Hampshire 03079
and by
MARION BOYARS Ltd.,
18 Brewer Street,
London W1R 4AS.

British Library Cataloging in Publication Data

Marowitz, Charles
Sex Wars: free adaptations of Ibsen and
Strindberg.
I. Title   II. Ibsen, Henrik.   Hedda Gabler
III. Ibsen, Henrik.   Enemy of the People
IV. Strindberg, August.
The Father
812'.54   PS3563.A68

ISBN 0-7145-2721-1
ISBN 0-7154-2722-X Pbk

Library of Congress Cataloging
in Publication Data

Marowitz, Charles.
Sex Wars.
I.   Ibsen, Henrik, 1828-1906. Hedda Gabler.
II.   Ibsen, Henrik, 1828-1906. Folkefiende.
III.   Strindberg, August, 1849-1912. Fadren.
IV.   Title.
PS3563.A68A6   812'.54   82-1133
ISBN 0-7145-2721-1   AACR2
ISBN 0-7145-2722-X (pbk.)

Printed in the United States of America
by Vail-Ballou Press, Inc., Binghamton, N.Y.

CONTENTS

Introduction

The only thing that links these two plays by Ibsen and the one by Strindberg is the fact that I was involved in their productions both in Norway and in England. It would be false to try to suggest, for the sake of some arbitrary continuity, that *Hedda Gabler, Enemy of the People* and *The Father* are in some way 'allied'. *Hedda* is a subtle character study whose ambiguities have long made it a favorite of leading actresses; *Enemy,* a kind of dramatized editorial written (one might almost say overwritten) in a fit of pique — possibly inspired by the adverse reception of *Ghosts. The Father* is a private hallucination disguised as a naturalistic drama and a work which shows Strindberg in his most obsessive and anti-feminist temper. *Hedda* was originally commissioned for Den Nationale Scene in Bergen; *Enemy* premiered at The National Theater in Oslo, and *The Father* presented at The Open Space Theater in London and subsequently at the Trondelag Theater in Trondheim.

Having firmly established the separateness of these three works, I would ask the reader to bear with me as I investigate certain affinities they seem to have in common; affinities which are as much tendencies in their authors and the social-psychological movement of the late nineteenth century as they are resemblances in the plays themselves. I should add that these affinities form part of the interpretation contained in the adaptations and are not necessarily in the author's original intentions; one being, in my view, quite separate from the other.

Hedda Gabler is in the world and not in it. She is in her society but not of it. She wants to transcend its gravitational tug and, in wanting this so intensely, can feel no real commitment to it. Nothing in 'the real world' is so efficacious it draws her out of her private world. Social circumstances are only firewood that enkindle personal fantasies.

Dr. Thomas Stockmann is in the world and not in it. He deliberately withdraws from society to work in its backwater and it is from that vantage-point that he hatches his plan to create the civic baths. When he is anti-social enough to try to shut them down because they have become polluted, he is cut off from society and relegated to its outer reaches. Nor is he put there only by others: he places himself there because of his refusal to share the values and priorities of his community. He is never at home in 'the real world', the world of the town, the citizens, the bureaucrats, the compromisers; and it is a kind of poetic justice that, not being part of that world, that world exiles him. Like Hedda, his transcendant spirit (both their temperaments are essentially radical) is punished for non-conformity.

The Captain in Strindberg's play is in the world but not in it. He is as remote from his garrison as if it were a lunar outpost. Although a cavalry officer, his instinct and inclination is towards research. He is a make-believe soldier and, as he admits, has turned to science to compensate for his disappointments in the army. He is part of the family, being its titular head, but not part of it, being the victim of its female conspiracies. He is as alienated in his home as ever Stockmann was in his besieged study or Hedda in the railway cars she was forced to share with Tesman. The Captain only feels at home in his mental universe where he can entertain no visitors, not even the Doctor who, one would have thought, might qualify as a colleague there. His terrors, induced to a certain extent by his wife but more so by his own isolation from the domesticity personified by the Nurse, Laura and Bertha, separate him entirely from what all other characters in the play would accept as 'the real world'.

The Captain is a casualty in the Sex War, valiantly fighting on to the bitter end. Hedda is a non-combatant in the Sex War preferring her fence-sitting neutrality to the cut-and-thrust that, for example, distinguishes Thea Elvstead. Dr. Stockmann is above the Sex War. He recognizes that it is only a skirmish in a much greater conflict between the defenders of the status quo (such as the Mayor, Aslaksen, Hovstad, Billing) and its opponents, himself and Petra. But in the relationship between father and daughter, there is a strong whiff of the Sex War. It is only when Petra rejects the illusions of her father that she scores a true victory for her sex. Until then, she is like every other father-dominated daughter, doting on principles she only dimly understands; a hostage in the Sex War.

Hedda, Stockmann and The Captain are all defeated in their respective conflicts. Reality always routs illusions and the Established Powers always punish those rebels who would try to make the world over in their own image. Hedda's psychosis, Stockmann's egotism and the Captain's paranoia all spring from the same intellectual source; a dissatisfaction with prevailing modes of thought and behavior and an unarticulated desire to change the world. The value of their respective ideas is less significant than the fact that in each case, society annihilates them. Bourgeois conventions, the Compact Majority and the Matriarchial Family are all allies. Between them, they hold all the winning cards. Against them, no one stands a chance.

C.M.

HEDDA

A Free Adaptation of Ibsen's "Hedda Gabler"

Based on a literal translation
by Joan Tindale

NOTES

A writer can no sooner prevent his deepest feelings from seeping into his work than he can prevent a cardiograph from recording the rhythm of his heatbeats. All good writing is charged with subterannean forces unconsciously discharged into the work of art which is itself, at best, only semi-conscious. Hence, the absurdity of *deciding* to write this or that. The external choices based on the conscious decision to write are as irrelevant to the final product as the dreams a person *decides* to have before going to sleep.

Hedda Gabler may not be specifically about the unrequited longings of an old man whose sexual instincts have been aroused by a young girl who threatens his emotional composure, but something of the dark hunger Ibsen felt for Emilie Bardach, who was 18 years old when he was 61, certainly trickled into the work. Similarly the resignation of a man who, in old age, acknowledges the disappearance of the reckless youth he used to be, does not figure obviously in the play, although I am certain it is at the root of Hedda's chronic disconsolateness. The play is full of mourning for lost opportunities, former times, previously held values, potentialities that once were and have now emptied themselves down the flues of routine and conformity. It is pervaded by the unmistakable aroma of death and what has died is something turbulent and independent in the author, unconsciously buried in the vault of his central character's personality. Hedda, despite her alleged 28 years, is ancient; the oldest character in modern drama. She emits the musty air of a stodgy old man who has been forced to accept the fact that comfort and success have been accompanied by compromise and the loss of something more precious than any of his tangible rewards. No, Ibsen did not shoot himself. 'People' like him 'don't do such things'. What they actually do, is contemplate the anguish of life which, because of some heedless timidity, some expedient decision, some seemingly inevitable yet actually avoidable choice, has made them squander the most precious thing in their life; the possibility of being true to their own nature no matter how dire the consequences to everyone else.

If ever one needed proof of Ibsen's misery, his sense of a life pathetically de-railed from its intended destination, *Hedda Gabler* provides it in abundance.

Hedda, like Hamlet, is in the throes of a passion in excess of her given circumstances. Her monumental *ennui* like the Prince's implacable melancholy, gushes from an inexhaustible fount at the center of her character. It submerges her personality. It is, in some palpable way, bound up with the universe. Hedda's tedium is an intensification of the tedium we all feel in the face of the unchangeableness of life; the inviolable structure of our unbending and unending social patterns. No wonder she longs for what Ibsen called 'the insuperable': for transcendence, for release. Her domicile is the dank, fetid, psychic dungeon in which we all conduct the listless business of our miserable lives. We are, all of us, hemmed in by respectable Aunt Julianas, chained to mediocrities like Tesman, taunted by opportunists like Brack and diverted by fantasies about overrated cult figures like Loevborg. But very few of us place a gun barrel in our mouths to savor the taste of mortality. Most of us nibble our mingy fish 'n chips and draw out our 'lives of quiet desperation'. Hedda, however, cannot settle for less. She is the kind of all-or-nothing person we rarely encounter in real life, hence our fascination for her in literature.

On the outside, Hedda is dull as ditchwater; a frustrated spouse, a gormless dreamer, a pointless flirt, a social snob in a social situation where the whole concept of 'snobbery' is ridiculous. Imagine a 'social snob' living in Hull dressing up in her best finery to impress the shopkeepers on the one night of the year when a gala concert occurs in the town hall. It's unthinkable! To have true social snobbery, you need a true society and in Hedda's dinky little town, there is no such thing. Brack is no gay Lothario; he's just a horny old bureaucrat. Give him a squalid massage-parlor and he is quite content. Give him an exotic cosmopolitan bordello and he wouldn't know what to ask for. And as for Loevborg, he might make a small reputation for himself in the little magazines, but if his work were ever reviewed by a major critic, it would be dealt with in one brief, dismissive paragraph.

Hedda is a spiritual outcast. She doesn't belong in a world that is committed to monotony. It's not so much that she was born ahead of her time for even today women are trapped by social rigidities (they exchange male chauvinist clichés for those of the women's liberation movement assuming that 'greater economic opportunity' in some way redresses the balance in the battle of the sexes). No period in history would be quite right for a woman like Hedda who hungers for an intensity of life which life almost never provides. It is not only that she is a coward (which she is) that makes her pathetic, for even if she were heroic, she would have nowhere to perform her heroics. The grind of petty existence would wear her down, just as it does the other rebellious malcontents who assume they are being prevented from pursuing a higher, richer life. What is of real interest in *Hedda Gabler* is not the character of the chief protagonist but the nature of the listless society which prevents her from realizing her smoldering potential. This is also what makes Hamlet interesting. What he could do if only the world corresponded to his idealized image of it! Instead, he converses with ghosts and rationalizes his weakness with comforting solliloquies just as Hedda seeks solace in day-dreams and empty romanticism.

HEDDA AND THEA: MALES AND FEMALES

Is Thea Elvstead a superior kind of Hedda Gabler?

Like Hedda, she is locked into a cloistered marriage with an incompatible older man. True, in Thea's case a *much* older man — but the temperamental gulf between Hedda and George Tesman is so great, it seems to suggest he is as far removed from his wife as Mr. Elvstead is from *his*.

Like Hedda, Thea longs for spiritual companionship with the opposite sex and a life with more meaning than that of the socially approved of housewife-cum-housekeeper, i.e. the 19th century married woman.

Like Hedda, she wants to control (partially if not entirely) the life of a man whose work has some social efficacy. Indeed, in the rivalry between Hedda and Thea, and despite the implicit superiority of Hedda's influence, it is Thea who wins Loevborg and with whom he enters into a practical collaboration; a living example of the kind of higher social affinities which he writes about (see Ibsen's notes *re* Loevborg and his manuscript.)

Like Hedda, she rejects the *ennui* of her preordained status and actively seeks alternatives to it. In Hedda's case, it is all surreptitious (flirtations with Brack and Loevborg); with Thea, it is entirely open (liaison with Loevborg; rejection of the Elvstead sanctum-of-security and all its attendant marital oppressions).

Unlike Thea who hungers for greater spiritual contact with an interesting man which doesn't stop short of sexual union, Hedda believes she wants what, ultimately, she cannot bear to possess, i.e. the consequences of true union with Loevborg; sexual interchange based on intellectual cameraderie. For all her 'wanting-to-know', Hedda is revealed to have the curiosity of the voyeur. She 'wants to know' for the sake of titilating her imagination, not conditioning her behavior. She questions Loevborg about his illicit activities with Diana and others because she wants (mentally) to wank; to indulge sensually in fantasies, the realities of which are forbidden to a 19th century woman of good family. But secretly, she accepts — even prefers — that denial. Like the sexual fantasist who comes to prefer his masturbations to the reality on which they are based, Hedda would rather live through Loevborg's experience than have the experience itself. Not only because 19th century social mores repress the woman who resists conformity, but also because there is a part of Hedda which is unalterably masculine; the part of her created and nurtured by the dominant father figure, General Gabler; the part of her which inclines her to equestrianism, pistols and manipulation of male admirers. It is not so far-fetched to suggest that in modern times, Hedda might be one of those women who seek out the sex-change operation in order to realize the swelling male potentialities in her nature; a drive very different from, and not to be confused with, latent lesbianism.

Does Hedda want (as she claims) the *frisson* which comes from the knowledge of forbidden experience in a man's world, or does she want the physiological sensation of maleness, and is the former the closest she can come to the latter? If that is the case, one must transcend the (now banal) feminist interpretation of Hedda as a repressed 19th century women's libber. It may well be society's fault that a woman is relegated to a lower sphere of activity, condemned to the kitchen and the nursery, the netherworld of marital drudgery. But is it also society's fault if a woman rejects her feminine temperament and pursues her genetic inclination, preferring the hardihood of male experience and the cut-and-thrust of male enterprises? Social repression can be laid at the door of the Social Repressors: the educators, the parents and the Church, but sexual repression which is more self-induced than environmentally-encouraged, is a very different matter.

MRS. GABLER

Of all the dramatic protagonists in history, the one most independent of a mother's influence is Hedda Gabler. An English essayist once asked sardonically: how many children did Lady Macbeth have? His answer was that, as far as Shakespeare's play was concerned, the question had no relevance whatsoever. By the same token, it is pointless to speculate on Hedda's mother. Was she a woman of easy virtue that the young Gabler encountered in his travels, fell in love with and with whom he sired Hedda? Was the moral laxity of this woman the reason why the General instilled such moral fervor into Hedda, giving her the fear of scandal which, next to sexual curiosity, is perhaps her strongest trait? Or was she perhaps a snivelling little *hausfrau* that the military man married early in his life and who died very soon after Hedda's birth, leaving the pale memory of an anonymous, socially-engulfed non-entity: the kind of woman Hedda secretly vowed never to become. Pointless speculation of course, and yet for an actress, these speculations pave the runway from which original characterizations take off. Is it then quite so pointless as the analytical mind insists? If a notion, an unfounded theory, a flight of fancy can be responsible for the graph of an entire dramatic characterization, should we not fill in every imaginative detail of these speculations? Or should we say, along with our sarcastic English essayist: it doesn't matter a damn how many children Lady Macbeth had!

COMEDIES AND TRAGEDIES:

The tragedy of Hedda Gabler is that in the 19th century, there was no such thing as Xerox copiers. Had there been a duplicate copy of Loevborg's manuscript, he would never have grown suicidal over its loss, equating it with the loss of his and Thea's child. He would never have come to Hedda distracted by what had happened and he would never have been induced to take Hedda's pistol and do away with himself. He would never have put Hedda into the predicament of giving him her pistol thereby placing her in the clutches of the blackmailing Judge Brack, ultimately compelling her to take her own life to avoid the loss of her freedom, the loss of Tesman's affection and the subjugation to Brack's will.

The debt we owe to the Rank Xerox Corporation we will never be able to pay.

RANDOM ENTRIES FROM THE DIARY OF HEDDA GABLER

Sept 3rd
It is autumn again. Closer to death. And yet I feel I have
not even begun to live. This town is like a halter around
my neck. The same listless faces, the same tedious greetings.
How I wish I could put them all into a great barge and
sink them in the fjord. I could always claim it was self-
defense. After all, they are destroying *me* day by day.

Sept 28th
Tesman called again today. How pathetic to see his love-
smitten face peering at me from behind the predictable
bouquet of roses. I loathe his attire. It is so correct. He
comes to collect me like a man about to call a meeting to
order. Still, they say his prospects are quite good . . . Why
is there always such unlimited scope for mediocrities? . . .
I made up an epigram today. The General didn't
understand it. Smoke goes up the chimney and disappears.
The coals that produce it stay below smoldering and
giving warmth. Eilert burns like coals. Tesman goes
straight up the chimney.

October 4th
Saw Eilert tonight. Alone. Father upstairs in the study. His
eyes were dark and ringed as if he had just journeyed
through hell. I felt his hunger for me like a dagger poking
through my dress. It does him good to hunger. Artists are
supposed to suffer, aren't they? I wonder what he would
feel like inside of me?

October 8th
Brack says if I'm not careful I'll wind up on the shelf. I'm
quite sure he would be the first to rescue me if I gave him
the chance. He finds every opportunity he can to brush up
against me. Oh quite innocently. I'm sure he has a short,
squat, wrinkled penis.

November 1st
Eilert has written me a sonnet. I was quite flattered when

he gave it to me and made a great fuss. Something about
Apollo and Aphrodite. I couldn't make head nor tail of it.

Nov 5th
The General has refused to let me ride for a whole
month . . . just because I took out his favorite stallion
without asking permission. But I'm having my revenge. I
sleep late every morning, pretending to have a headache
and he has to prepare his own breakfast. How petty he can
be!

Dec 14th
Tesman is growing more and more intense. He calls twice
a week now and the roses grow bigger each time. Since
Eilert is otherwise occupied (God knows where, and with
whom?), it passes the time. I'm sure the news will soon get
back to him and he'll come running back — although this
time he won't find me as he left me . . . He thinks just
because he is swarthy and handsome . . . They say George
Tesman may become a professor. Imagine, a professor's
wife! How I would turn the young students' heads. If they
were naughty, I'd have to keep them after class. That
could be quite fun.

Dec 18th
How I wish Eilert would come back. Tesman is driving me
quite mad with his flowers and his 'sentiments'. Even
Brack is a relief. If only he wouldn't keep his eyes fixed on
my bodice while making conversation.

Dec 20th
There is a 'me' that no one knows, not even the General.
I'm a little frightened to know her myself. Still, if we were
all saints, this would be heaven and God knows, whatever
it is, it isn't that.

January 4th
Tesman has proposed.
What is the difference being alone with another or being
alone by oneself?

CAST

HEDDA GABLER
GENERAL GABLER
EILERT LOEVBORG
GEORGE TESMAN
JUDGE BRACK
THEA ELVSTEAD
MISS JULIANA TESMAN
AUNT RENA
BERTHA
MADEMOISELLE DIANA
TWO PROSTITUTES
TWO POLICEMEN

Lights up

GENERAL GABLER, *an imposing figure in
uniform, staring sternly down-stage right.*

Lights up down-stage right.

HEDDA *stiff, cowering. The* GENERAL *gesturing
with one finger, orders his daughter to stand before
him. Cautiously, she moves to the* GENERAL,
places herself before him and kneels. The GENERAL
snaps his fingers and opens his hand, asking for
HEDDA's *hand. Tentatively,* HEDDA *stretches out
her right hand, placing the other, with fist clenched,
behind her back. The* GENERAL *takes leather
gloves from his belt and raps* HEDDA's *hands three
times.* HEDDA's *back tightens with each blow. We
cannot see her face. After the third blow, the*
GENERAL *replaces his gloves and* HEDDA *rises.*

The GENERAL *opens his arms wide and, tentatively,*
HEDDA *enters the* GENERAL's *embrace. As she
turns her head within the* GENERAL's *bosom, we
see a hard, unrepentant face which in no way returns
the affection being offered by her father.* HEDDA
looks grimly out to the AUDIENCE.

Lights fade.

Blackout.

Lights out.

HEDDA *astride the* GENERAL's *shoulders. The*
GENERAL *strides around the stage giving* HEDDA
a 'piggy-back' ride. HEDDA *is clearly enjoying this.*

She eggs on her mount to go faster and faster — he does so. She whips him with her riding crop. He attempts to go even faster, cannot, and finally slumps to his knees. Irritably, HEDDA dismounts. The GENERAL, out of breath, puts one hand to his throat and beckons HEDDA with his other hand as if asking for refreshment.

HEDDA pushes him aside, causing the GENERAL to slump even lower onto his knees. Trying to rise, he gestures for help. HEDDA slaps him sharply across the forehead with her riding crop, and walks away. The GENERAL, still on his knees, breathless and in need of help.

Slow fade out.

Lights up.

As before on the GENERAL standing rock solid and sternly facing down stage right.

Lights up.

On HEDDA, as before.

The two characters confront each other, HEDDA trying to be firm but revealing her trepidation; the GENERAL, stern and implacable.

Fade out.

Lights up.

HEDDA now standing center, in the General's former position, facing down stage right, cool, calm and collected.

Lights up.

On EILERT LOEVBERG.

LOEVBORG: *(slowly, with deep feeling)* Hedda . . .
Hedda Gabler.

HEDDA: Ssh!

LOEVBORG: *(repeats softly)* Hedda Gabler.

HEDDA: That used to be my name. When we first
knew each other.

LOEVBORG: And from now on — for the rest of my
life — I must stop myself from saying, 'Hedda
Gabler'.

HEDDA: Yes, you must. You'd better get used to it.
The sooner the better.

TESMAN: *(appearing at her opposite side)* What are
you looking at Hedda?

HEDDA: Only the leaves. They're so yellow and
withered.

TESMAN: It is September.

HEDDA: September. Already.

LOEVBORG: Hedda Gabler married. And to George
Tesman!

TESMAN: Auntie Yulie was behaving peculiarly, I
thought, didn't you? Do you know what got into
her?

HEDDA: I hardly know her. Isn't she always like that?

TESMAN: Not the way she was today.

LOEVBORG: Oh Hedda, Hedda . . . how could you?

HEDDA: Oh, I shall make it up with her soon enough.

TESMAN: Oh Hedda, would you?

HEDDA: Ask her to drop by here one evening, when you see her again.

TESMAN: Oh that *would* be nice, Hedda. You know, there's another thing that would make her pleased as punch.

HEDDA: Yes?

TESMAN: If you could bring yourself to call her Auntie Yulie

LOEVBORG: How could you throw yourself away like that?

HEDDA: *(to LOEVBORG, sharply)* Stop it! *(equally sharply to TESMAN)* Really, Tesman, you mustn't ask me things like that. I've told you I'll call her Aunt Juliana, and that will have to do!

LOEVBORG: Tell me Hedda. How could you do it?

HEDDA: If you go on calling me Hedda, I simply won't answer.

TESMAN: Is anything wrong, Hedda?

HEDDA: *(aimlessly to TESMAN)* I was just looking at my old piano.

LOEVBORG: Not even when we're alone?

HEDDA: It doesn't go with everything else, really.

TESMAN: As soon as my salary starts, we'll see about getting it replaced.

LOEVBORG: Not even then?

HEDDA: *(flirtatiously)* No. You can think it, but you mustn't say it.

BRACK: *(appearing)* Oh, I see. Because of your deep love for George Tesman, I suppose.

HEDDA: *(turning to BRACK)* Don't use that soppy word.

BRACK: *(mock shock)* But Mrs. Hedda . . .

HEDDA: *(irritably)* What are all those books you've got there?

TESMAN: The latest publications dealing with my dissertation.

HEDDA: Your dissertation?

TESMAN: The Domestic Industries of Brabant in the Middle Ages.

HEDDA: *(to BRACK)* You try it for awhile, Judge. Getting the history of civilization shoved down your throat morning, noon and . . .

LOEVBORG: *(questioning)* You don't love him?

BRACK: But if you feel like that, why . . .

HEDDA: Did I marry George Tesman?

LOEVBORG: *(declaring)* You don't love him!

HEDDA: *(to LOVEBORG)* I've no intention of being unfaithful — if that's what you're hinting.

BRACK: But Mrs. Hedda . . .

HEDDA: I'd danced myself out, Judge. I felt my number was up.

LOEVBORG: *(solicitously)* No, you mustn't say that. Or even think it.

BRACK: You've no reason to think it.

HEDDA: *(regarding TESMAN)* After all, George Tesman, well, I mean, he's quite upstanding, isn't he?

TESMAN: *(of himself as if in a mirror)* Very upstanding. Thoroughly respectable. No doubt about that.

MISS TESMAN: *(appearing with BERTHA, umbilically tied to her)* He's been made a doctor, Bertha. By some foreigners.

BERTHA: Imagine little George, tending the sick.

MISS TESMAN: *(irritated)* Not that kind of doctor. *(to George)* Oh George, you are so clever.

TESMAN: *(to MISS TESMAN and BERTHA)* I
  imagine there are quite a few people in this town
  who wouldn't mind being in my shoes.

MISS TESMAN: *(admiringly)* The Domestic
  Industries of Brabant in the Middle Ages.

BERTHA: Ey?

MISS TESMAN: *(explaining irritably)* The title of his
  dissertation!

TESMAN: Of course it will take a little while before I
  actually get down to it. There are all these notes to
  be indexed and cross-indexed, filed and cross-filed,
  memoranda, addenda; that kind of thing.

HEDDA: *(studying him with BRACK)* There's nothing
  obviously ridiculous about him?

TESMAN: *(pride stung)* Ridiculous?

MISS TESMAN: *(studying him)* No, I wouldn't say
  that.

BERTHA: He's very clever at making notes and all
  that kind of thing.

BRACK: *(studying him)* He may go quite far. One can
  never tell.

TESMAN: *(to MISS TESMAN)* There's every reason
  to believe that before long, I shall have acquired
  the status of a full professor.

MISS TESMAN: A professor!

TESMAN: One might almost say it's a fait accompli.

BERTHA: He could be anything he likes, little
      Georgie.

TESMAN: I'm really looking forward to getting down
      to it. Especially now that I've got a home of my
      own.

MISS TESMAN: Oh George, imagine, a married
      man! And to think it's you who's carried off Hedda
      Gabler.

LOEVBORG: *(lovingly)* The beautiful Hedda
      Gabler.

BERTHA: I never dreamed I'd live to see a match
      between her and little Georgie.

MISS TESMAN: You must stop calling him 'little
      Georgie'!

BERTHA: That new girl! She'll never learn to do
      things properly . . .

MISS TESMAN: I'll train her up all right. *(back to
      TESMAN)* She was always admired; surrounded by
      suitors.

BRACK: *(fondly)* I've been longing for you to get
      back.

HEDDA: Not as much as I.

BRACK: *(surprised)* Really Mrs. Hedda? And I
      imagined you were having such a marvellous
      honeymoon.

MISS TESMAN: *(hinting)* I'm sure you didn't waste a
      single moment of *your* honeymoon.

BERTHA: Not our little Georgie.

HEDDA: *(sardonically)* Oh just marvellous.

TESMAN: I filled whole books with notes for my dissertation. It's incredible what you can turn up rooting around in old archives. Amazing things that no one ever dreamt were there.

MISS TESMAN: *(enthusiastically)* And what a honeymoon! Five whole months!

HEDDA: *(bored)* Nearly six.

BRACK: But your husband sent back such rhapsodic letters.

HEDDA: He thinks.

TESMAN: *(soberly to MISS TESMAN)* 'The most satisfying thing in the world is browsing through libraries and copying out precious pieces of parchment . . .'

HEDDA: *(throwaway)* Or whatever it is he does.

MISS TESMAN: *(defensive to HEDDA)* Well that *is* his life. A good part of it anyway. *(To George)* But tell me, George, don't you have some extra little news for us?

TESMAN: *(Slyly)* Have you noticed how plump and rosy she's looking? How she's filled out in one or two places.

MISS TESMAN: Filled out?

BERTHA: *(the know-it-all)* I was afraid that would
            happen.

HEDDA: Shall we change the subject.

TESMAN: Oh yes, Auntie Yulie, you can 't see it too
            clearly in that dress, but I can tell you on good
            authority . . .

HEDDA: *(to TESMAN)* You can't tell anyone
            anything! *(to BRACK)* Oh no, my dear Judge, the
            fact is, I have been utterly bored to death.

TESMAN: *(hearing it)* Do you really mean that?

HEDDA: *(to TESMAN, defiantly)* Yes.

            TESMAN and AUNT depart in a huff.

            (to BRACK) Just picture it, Judge. Six whole
            months without meeting a single person who was
            remotely one of us and with whom I could hold a
            conversation on a subject of mutual interest.

LOEVBORG: Didn't you love me either? Not even a
            little?

HEDDA: *(to LOEVBORG)* You certainly opened
            your heart to me.

LOEVBORG: You begged me to.

HEDDA: And there was something touching and
            tender and exciting about the way we confided in
            each other. That deep and intimate friendship that
            no one else even guessed at.

BRACK: *(cutting in)* Yes, well now *we* can enjoy a nice, cosy little chat, Mrs Hedda.

HEDDA: It seems an eternity since we talked.

LOEVBORG: You remember how I'd come up to your father's house in the afternoon with the General sitting by the window with his back towards us reading his newspaper . . .

HEDDA: The two of us on the sofa in the corner.

BRACK: *(coming between them)* It's very pleasant you know, to have a small circle of friends whom I can assist in one way or another . . .

LOEVBORG: *(close to HEDDA)* Always thumbing the same picture magazine . . .

BRACK: . . . and into whose house I may freely come and go like a good and trusted friend.

HEDDA: *(With LOEVBORG)* Of the husband?

BRACK: Preferably, to be quite frank, of the wife.

LOEVBORG: Imparting secrets to you long into the night . . .

BRACK: And of the husband too, of course.

LOEVBORG: Telling you things about myself that I never dared admit to anyone else. Those miserable days and nights of drinking and debauchery. Oh Hedda, what power did you have to make me confess such things?

HEDDA: *(to THEA)* Power?

THEA: *(who has just appeared)* It happened quite
          gradually. I seemed to develop a kind of power
          over him.

HEDDA: *(to THEA)* Oh? *(To Loevborg)* You think I
          had some power over you?

LOEVBORG: How else can one explain it?

THEA: He came to see us every day to give the
          children lessons. Gradually, he began to give up his
          old habits. Not because I asked him to. I'd never
          had dared do that. I suppose he came to realize
          that kind of thing offended me and so, little by
          little, he just stopped.

HEDDA: So it was you who salvaged the unsalvageable
          Eilert Loevborg. Clever little Thea.

BRACK: *(in close contact with HEDDA)* You know,
          that kind of triangular relationship is a perfect
          arrangement for all concerned.

HEDDA: *(intimately to BRACK)* How I longed for a
          third party to intrude. All those dreary hours in
          dusty railway cars.

LOEVBORG: And all those indelicate questions you
          kept asking.

HEDDA: *(to LOEVBORG but toying with BRACK)*
          You answered them quite readily, as I recall.

THEA: He's made a whole person out of me. Taught
          me to use my mind, to question all kinds of things.

HEDDA: *(sarcastic)* Gave *you* lessons as well, did he?

LOEVBORG: *(with HEDDA)* That you had the audacity to ask such questions. So shamelessly.

THEA: *(Combative to HEDDA)* He talked to me! Really talked. About every thing imaginable. And then, we began to work together. It was wonderful. To help him. To be allowed to help him.

HEDDA: You don't sound very sure of him.

THEA: Something stands between Eilert Loevborg and me. The memory of some other woman.

HEDDA: Who can that be?

LOEVBORG: *(to HEDDA)* Someone he's never been able to forget.

THEA: He said when they parted she tried to shoot him with a pistol.

LOEVBORG: How absurd. *(clammy)* People don't do such things.

BRACK: *(Close, hot)* Thankfully, your honeymoon is now over.

HEDDA: There's still some way to go. I'm only a stop along the line.

BRACK: *(hot)* That's the time to jump out and stretch your legs a bit, Mrs. Hedda.

LOEVBORG: *(serious)* That you could dare to ask me about such things . . .

HEDDA: I'm not the type to jump.

BRACK: *(hot)* Aren't you?

HEDDA: No. There's always someone around who . . .

LOEVBORG: *(obscenely flirtatious)* Looks up your skirts.

HEDDA: Exactly.

BRACK: But just consider Hedda . . .

HEDDA: *(breaking away from both — Going towards TESMAN)* No thank you! I prefer to stay where I am. Sitting together in the compartment.

BRACK: *(rebuffed, trying again)* But suppose someone were to join you in the compartment.

HEDDA: What sort of someone?

LOEVBORG: A cosy friend . . . a good comrade . . .

THEA: Comrade, yes. That's just the word he used.

BRACK: Who was kind and understood . . .

THEA: All kinds of things!

LOEVBORG: And was lively?

HEDDA: And amusing?

BRACK: And in no way dry or academic . . .

HEDDA: That'd be a change.

LOEVBORG: Tell me Hedda what did you feel for me?

HEDDA: *(breaking away from all)* Why is it so incredible that a young girl, given the opportunity, wouldn't peer into that forbidden world of whose existence she is supposed to be ignorant. Everything had been kept from me. I had a craving to know. Everything!

LOEVBORG: You never loved me.

BRACK: *(rebuffed)* Oh *I* never really entertained any hopes of you.

LOEVBORG: You just wanted . . .

HEDDA: To know!

LOEVBORG: If that was so, then why did you break it off?

HEDDA: Because your friendship was threatening to develop into something — something much more serious. Shame on you Eilert Loevborg. How could you stoop to take advantage of a good, unsuspecting comrade. Well, it doesn't matter now, does it? You've found your consolation at the Elvsteads.

LOEVBORG: I know you've got Thea to confide in you.

HEDDA: And you confided in her, no doubt.

LOEVBORG: Not a word. She's too stupid to understand that kind of thing.

THEA: *(stung)* Stupid?

LOEVBORG: You are stupid about that kind of thing.

THEA: Eilert dear, please listen to me . . .

LOEVBORG: Why didn't you do it? Why didn't you finish me off when you had the chance?

BRACK: Terrified of the scandal! Yes Hedda, you've always been a coward at heart. *(decisively to TESMAN)* My dear Tesman, there is something I feel you ought to know and the sooner the better.

TESMAN: Concerning Eilert?

BRACK: Concerning him and you.

THEA: *(star struck)* I've just got your new book though I haven't read it through, of course.

LOEVBORG: *(transferring affections to THEA)* This is my true book. *(with MS)* The one that truly expresses me.

THEA: *(flattered)* Really, what's it about?

BRACK: Your nomination might not come through quite as soon as you might expect.

LOEVBORG: It's the sequel.

THEA: To what?

TESMAN: Is anything wrong?

LOEVBORG: To the other book.

THEA: The one that's just appeared.

LOEVBORG: Yes.

TESMAN: *(distracted from BRACK)* But my dear Eilert, that treats the subject right up to the present.

LOEVBORG: And this one's about the future.

THEA: The future. But we don't know anything about that.

LOEVBORG: Perhaps not, but there are still one or two things to be said about it. *(Hands MS to TESMAN)* Look it over, Tesman.

BRACK: The appointment may well be decided by competition.

TESMAN: *(to BRACK)* Competition?

HEDDA: Imagine that.

TESMAN: But who else . . . I mean . . . you don't mean that . . .

THEA: *(staunch supporter)* Exactly. By competition with Eilert Loevborg.

LOEVBORG: It's in two parts. The first deals with the cultural forces that are shaping our civilization . . .

TESMAN: *(outraged)* Incredible!

LOEVBORG: And the second about the way in
    which that civilization may develop.

HEDDA: *(accusingly with MS)* That's not your
    handwriting.

LOEVBORG: It was dictated.

THEA: *(springing to his defence)* Whenever he wrote
    anything, we always did it together.

HEDDA: *(catty)* Like two good comrades!

THEA: Yes. That's just the word he used.

TESMAN: *(to BRACK)* But this is inconceivable. It's
    just . . . impossible!

LOEVBORG: It may well happen nevertheless.

TESMAN: That would be extremely inconsiderate.
    I'm a married man. It was on the strength of this
    position that I *got* married.

MISS TESMAN: No need to get so worked up,
    George. It's only a formality.

TESMAN: That annuity's all you and Aunt Rena have
    in the world.

MISS TESMAN: I've stood security for all the
    furniture and carpets.

TESMAN: *(aghast)* You stood security?

MISS TESMAN: It's just a formality. Judge Brack
    told me so. You'll have a salary of your own now.

TESMAN: *(to BRACK)* We've run up some pretty hefty debts. Borrowed a great deal of money.

MISS TESMAN: *(oblivious)* It's just wonderful how everything's working out so well.

TESMAN: I mean, Good God, they practically guaranteed me that job.

MISS TESMAN: And the enemies who tried to oppose you have fallen by the wayside; completely vanquished. And he who was your most dangerous rival has had the greatest fall. He made his bed and now he's got to lie in it, poor misguided creature.

TESMAN: Auntie Yulie, are you completely off your head?

BRACK: *(wrapping it up)* There, there — no doubt you'll get it in the end.

THEA: *(catty)* But first you'll have to compete. *(to TESMAN)* I've got hold of Eilert Loevborg's latest book. *(to HEDDA)* Would you like to see it?

HEDDA: *(tossing book aside; starting to stalk TESMAN)* You said we would enter society; entertain lavishly. That was the agreement.

THEA: *(baiting them both)* It's remarkably well written. A real feat.

TESMAN: *(lamely)* I was hoping we would. I was looking forward to you playing the hostess, having a select circle.

BERTHA: Oh she's a real lady, you can see that.

MISS TESMAN: *(to BERTHA)* General Gabler's
     daughter.

THEA: *(with pride)* He never wrote like that before.

MISS TESMAN: Do you remember?

BERTHA: As if anyone could forget.

MISS TESMAN: How she used to ride out with her
     father.

THEA: Everyone's praising it.

LOEVBORG: It was intended to be popular.

TESMAN: But for a while, we'll have to make do with
     our own company.

BRACK: Spending every minute of one's life with the
     same person. Tch, tch, tch . . .

HEDDA: Without a liveried servant?

TESMAN: We couldn't possibly afford that.

MISS TESMAN: In a long black dress.

HEDDA: And the black stallion you promised me?

TESMAN: Stallion?

MISS TESMAN: With a feather in her hat.

HEDDA: I must forget all of that now, mustn't I?

THEA: *(spiteful)* You're both studying the same
     subject, are you not?

TESMAN: *(of HEDDA's line)* Heaven forbid.

BRACK: You're both in the same field.

LOEVBORG: *(superior)* Well, we used to be.

MISS TESMAN: *(admiringly)* Beautiful . . . beautiful.

> *HEDDA suddenly pulls MISS TESMAN's straw hat down over her ears.*

HEDDA: At least there's one thing I've still to do to amuse myself with.

TESMAN: *(shaking)* What's that Hedda?

HEDDA: My pistols, George darling.

TESMAN:
BRACK: *(together)* Pistols!
LOEVBORG:

HEDDA: General Gabler's pistols!

> *Giant pistol suddenly appears from above. HEDDA mounts it and begins to spin upon it, threatening all about her. Simultaneous with this, GENERAL GABLER appears with real pistols cocked, and as HEDDA threatens all with giant pistol, GABLER goes haywire with the actual pistols, shooting on every side. ALL flee to escape GEN. GABLER's pistol-shot and HEDDA's range of fire. Things subside. Pistol disappears.*

> *HEDDA and THEA are left together.*

> *Lights dim slightly.*

HEDDA: Well now, we've killed two birds with one stone.

THEA: What do you mean?

HEDDA: Didn't you sense I wanted to get rid of him so we could speak to each other alone.

THEA: But there's nothing more to tell, Mrs. Tesman. Really not.

HEDDA: Of course there is. Lots more. I can see that. Come along now, let's sit down and have a little chat.

THEA: I really ought to be going.

HEDDA: Oh there's no hurry, surely. Well. How have things been at home?

THEA: That's the last thing I wish to discuss.

HEDDA: Surely you can tell me. Good heavens, we did go to school together.

THEA: But you were a year above me. I was terribly frightened of you in those days.

HEDDA: *(losing years)* Frightened of me?

THEA: Yes, terribly, When you passed me on the stairs, you used to pull my hair.

HEDDA: *(losing years)* No. Did I really?

THEA: *(losing years)* Yes, and you once said you'd burn it all off.

HEDDA: I was joking. You must've known that.

THEA: *(a child)* I was so stupid in those days.

HEDDA: *(a child)* Why, we used to call each other by our first names at school.

THEA: I don't think so.

HEDDA: *(slaps her)* Of course we did! I remember it very well. *(suddenly chumy)* We should tell each other all our secrets — just like we used to. *(Kisses her; THEA withdraws)* There now. You must call me Hedda.

THEA: *(slowly)* Hedda.

HEDDA: *(kisses her)* That's right.

THEA: Oh, you're so kind.

HEDDA: And I'll call you Tora, just like I used to.

THEA: My name is Thea.

HEDDA: *(slaps her)* I *meant* Thea.

THEA cowers.

You went to Mrs. Elvstead as a housekeeper didn't you?

THEA: Governess. But his wife got very ill and had to spend all her time in bed, so I had to look after the house too.

HEDDA: But then you became the mistress, didn't you?

THEA: Yes, I did.

HEDDA: How long ago was that?

THEA: About five years. Oh, those five years. Especially the last two or three, if you only knew, Mrs. Tesman.

HEDDA: *(slaps her hard)* Mrs. Tesman?

THEA: *(cowering)* Hedda. I'm sorry. I'll try to remember. If you only knew what I . . .

HEDDA: *(rising)* Eilert Loevborg was up there too for a while, wasn't he?

THEA: *(maturing discernibly)* Eilert Loevborg?

HEDDA: Did you know him before? From town?

THEA: No, not really. I knew him by name, of course.

HEDDA: While you were there, he came quite often to the house.

THEA: Almost every day. To give lessons to the children. Managing the house was a full time job. I couldn't do that as well.

HEDDA: Of course you couldn't. And your husband. I suppose has to travel a good deal.

THEA: Yes, being a bailiff, he has to be all over the district so he's away most of the time.

HEDDA: *(taking her round)* Poor, pretty little Thea. Now you must tell me the whole story. From the beginning. Just the way it is.

THEA: What do you want to know?

HEDDA: What's your husband really like? Is he good to you?

THEA: He does his best, I suppose.

HEDDA: Surely he's much too old for you, isn't he?

THEA: (*outburst*) Oh, it's all too much for me. We have nothing in common. Nothing. We don't agree on anything. It's all become so horrid.

HEDDA: But surely he loves you . . . in his own way.

THEA: I'm a convenience. I don't cost much to keep. I'm just cheap labor.

HEDDA: That's a silly thing to say.

THEA: You don't know. He's not capable of loving anyone but himself.

HEDDA: And Eilert Loevborg. He must care a little about him.

THEA: (*neutral*) Eilert Loevborg? What makes you say that?

HEDDA: To send you all the way into town to look for him. Besides, you said as much to Tesman a moment ago.

THEA: (*maturing*) Did I? Maybe I did. I might as well tell you the whole story. It's bound to come out sooner or later.

HEDDA: *(maturing)* My dear Thea . . .

THEA: My husband had no idea I was leaving.

HEDDA: You didn't tell him?

THEA: He wasn't even at home. He's always away
           somewhere or other. I couldn't stand it any longer,
           Hedda. It was so terribly lonely up there.

HEDDA: And so you . . .

THEA: Packed my things. Secretly. And left.

HEDDA: Just like that?

THEA: I caught the first train and came straight
           down.

HEDDA: But my dear Thea, how did you dare to do
           it?

THEA: What else could I do?

HEDDA: But what will your husband say when you
           return?

THEA: Return? To him?

HEDDA: Surely you'll . . .

THEA: I shall never go back there again.

HEDDA: You mean . . . you've left for good?

THEA: There was nothing else I could do.

HEDDA: You just left. Like that?

THEA: There's no point in hiding something like that.

HEDDA: But what will people say when they . . .

THEA: Whatever they like. There was no alternative.

HEDDA: What will happen now. How will you live?

THEA: I don't know. I only know I must be where Eilert Loevborg is. If I'm to live at all.

There is a pause during which HEDDA, who has listened bitterly to the last speech, visibly dwindles down to a child again. THEA, watching her, slowly does likewise.

When the transformation has taken place, THEA begins to cower, sensing a growing threat. HEDDA's evil intentions to THEA slowly build, then suddenly, without warning, she makes a grab for THEA, takes hold of her hair and cruelly pulls it from her scalp. THEA screeches like a terrified child.

LOEVBORG enters.

THEA runs into LOEVBORG's arms. HEDDA stands glowering at both of them.

HEDDA: *(with BRACK and TESMAN suddenly behind her)* Well gentlemen. Shall we all go in and have a glass of cold punch?

BRACK: Good idea. One for the road.

TESMAN: Excellent, Hedda. Excellent.

ALL confront LOEVBORG and THEA.

HEDDA: Do have a drop, Mr. Loevborg.
           Pause.

LOEVBORG: No thank you. Not for me.

BRACK: Great heavens, man, cold punch isn't
           poison.

LOEVBORG: Not for everyone, perhaps.

BRACK: *(after a thought)* You could bring your
           manuscript and read it aloud to both of us.

TESMAN: Excellent idea.

BRACK: I have plenty of space.

           Pause.

           They ALL stand, still confronting each other.

HEDDA: Thea, darling, how about you. You'll join
           us in a glass of punch.

THEA: No thank you. I never drink that sort of thing.

HEDDA: Mr. Loevborg?

LOEVBORG: No thank you.

THEA: Neither does he.

HEDDA: Not even if I were to ask you especially . . .

LOEVBORG: Not even then.

HEDDA: So I have no power over you whatsoever.

LOEVBORG: Not where this is concerned.

HEDDA: Still. I really think you should. For your own sake.

THEA: Hedda!

LOEVBORG: And what is that supposed to mean?

HEDDA: Or perhaps I should say, for the sake of others.

LOEVBORG: Oh?

HEDDA: People might feel you weren't quite sure of yourself. Deep down.

LOEVBORG: People can think what they like.

BRACK: Firm as a rock.

TESMAN: A man of principle!

BRACK: Quite right, too.

   Beat

HEDDA: There, didn't I tell you so this morning when you were so hysterical . . .

LOEVBORG: Hysterical?

THEA: Hedda!

HEDDA: See for yourself. There's no need to be so frightened just because . . . In any case, let's all cheer up and enjoy ourselves.

After a cold, cruel look to THEA, LOEVBORG turns to BRACK.

LOEVBORG: *(to Brack)* You were good enough to ask me to join you.

THEA: *(interceding)* Eilert . . .

BERTHA gives out glasses.

As LOEVBORG begins the next speech, BRACK, TESMAN & HEDDA pour punch from decanter into glasses and then back again — as in a ceremony.

During this ceremony, LOEVBORG's speech gets slurred and he becomes progressively inebriated.

LOEVBORG: So that was how much faith you had in your 'comrade'? Did your husband send you after me to fetch me back? I suppose he needed an extra hand at the card table. Did you and he consult to make sure I wouldn't cause anyone any embarrassment? That wouldn't do, would it. Not at all. Well let's drink to the old man. To him. And to you.

BRACK: *(taking LOEVBORG round the shoulder as well as TESMAN. All three staggering and drunk)* Ladies and Gentlemen, the festivities have begun. I trust we shall all have a jolly old time and, as a lady of my acquaintance is wont to say, good hunting. Good night ladies, good night.

ALL stagger out.

HEDDA stands as if intoxicated herself, facing out.

GENERAL GABLER appears behind her.

GABLER: Hedda. Hedda. How will all this end?

HEDDA: At ten o'clock. That's when he'll come. I can see him clearly. Passionate. Shameless. With vine-leaves in his hair.

GABLER: *(shaking his head)* Hedda, Hedda.

HEDDA: You can doubt him as much as you like. I believe in him.

GABLER: You want something, Hedda. I can see it in your eyes.

HEDDA: Yes I do. For once in my life I want power over another human being; to shape him to my will, to hold him in the palm of my hand.

GABLER: You already have that power.

HEDDA: I haven't. I've never had it.

GABLER: Not even with your husband?

HEDDA: Him? That wouldn't be worth having. Oh, if you only knew how poor I am.

Lights change.

GABLER disappears.

THEA re-appears.

And you . . . you're allowed to be so rich, so rich.

*HEDDA embraces THEA and runs her fingers
through her hair.*

I think I will burn your hair off, after all.

> *THEA screams and backs away as MISS TESMAN
> — dressed now as GEORGE TESMAN — walks
> between them holding books under her arm.*

> *THEA drops down on side of the stage and sleeps.*

MISS TESMAN: *(carrying in books)* I'd better get on
with all this.

HEDDA: *(irritated at the interruption)* What are all
those books?

MISS TESMAN: The latest works for my dissertation.

HEDDA: Your dissertation? Haven't you collected
enough books for your dissertation.

MISS TESMAN: One can never have too many,
Hedda. One must keep abreast of everything that's
published on the subject. Absolutely everything.

HEDDA: *(sarcastically)* Absolutely.

MISS TESMAN: I've got hold of Eilert Loevborg's
new book as well. Would you like a loan of it,
Hedda?

HEDDA: No thank you very much.

MISS TESMAN: I was browsing through it on the way
home.

HEDDA: And what's your considered opinion?

MISS TESMAN: It's sound. Very sound. He never wrote like that before. Never. Well, I better get on with these right away. It will be such a pleasure to cut the pages and . . . Oh, by the way, Auntie Yulie won't be coming this evening after all.

HEDDA: Oh. All that hat business I suppose.

MISS TESMAN: Good heavens, no. How could you think that of Aunt Yulie. No, it's just that Auntie Rena's feeling very poorly.

TESMAN wheels in wheelchair with AUNT RENA, sickly and white seated in it.

MISS TESMAN: I'm afraid she's never going to mend entirely, poor dear. She just lies there as she has for years. Pray God, I'll be able to keep her a little while longer. If she passed on, I don't know what I'd do. *(turns to HEDDA)* But you can't imagine how pleased Auntie Yulie was that you looked so well after the honeymoon. Oh, she was just beaming with pleasure, Hedda. We all were. *(goes to wheelchair with TESMAN)*

HEDDA: *(taking hold of wheelchair and pushing it into wings)* Oh these eternal and everlasting Aunts!

TESMAN appears, looks sympathetically at HEDDA and begins to comfort her.

She pulls away.

TESMAN: *(covering up his rejection)* You're not really happy.

HEDDA: Can you give me one single reason why I should be?

TESMAN: This house. You once told me that, more
than anything else, you wanted to live here. The
house that first drew us together. Now it's been so
beautifully done up and turned into a home.

HEDDA: There's a stench of lavender and dried roses
in all the rooms. Aunt Juliana's doing, no doubt.

TESMAN: Hedda.

HEDDA: There's the smell of death over everything.
It reminds me of the flowers one has worn at a ball
— the morning after. How shall I while away the
evenings here? Can you imagine how bored I'm
going to be. How insufferably bored.

MISS TESMAN: *(appearing)* I shall come and visit
every day. Both of you. Every single day.

*HEDDA, frightened by the proximity, turns from
MISS TESMAN to find AUNT RENA and BERTHA
bearing down on her. She stops. They stop.*

An old Norwegian folk-tune starts up.

MISS TESMAN: *(during the dance)* Well, Bertha,
dear, now you've got yourself a new mistress.
Heaven knows, it breaks my heart to have to part
with you.

BERTHA: How do you think I feel? After all those
happy years I've spent with you and Miss Rena.

MISS TESMAN: *(dancing)* We must take it all in our
stride, Bertha. It's the only way. But George still
needs you to look after him. He couldn't cope
without you, you know.

AUNT RENA: We've cared for him since he was almost in diapers.

BERTHA: If only poor Joachim could rise out of his grave and see what little George has grown into.

TESMAN joins the dance.

HEDDA tries to duck out, but the dance brings her back into the group where she is partnered with TESMAN.

BERTHA: *(dancing)* I'm afraid the new mistress is not too pleased with me.

AUNT RENA: Nonsense, Bertha.

BERTHA: She's so refined. A real lady. Wants everything just so.

HEDDA finally breaks away from the dance and confronts them all like a caged animal. They stand watching her coldly: expressionless.

TESMAN turns to MISS TESMAN, MISS TESMAN to AUNT RENA, AUNT RENA to BERTHA who approaches HEDDA quietly, ominously.

BERTHA: *(playing the dutiful servant)* Did you require anything, madam.

HEDDA: *(frightened: regards them all)* It's chilly. Put some more logs on the fire.

BERTHA: *(looks to others as if sharing a secret)* Now, don't you fret. I'll soon have this house warm as toast.

MISS TESMAN makes sound of front door bell.

Someone's at the front door, madam.

HEDDA: Well go and see to it.

BERTHA: But the fire . . .

HEDDA: *(impatient)* I'll tend to that myself.

BERTHA: *(smiling slyly to others)* It'll soon heat up, madame. You'll see.

HEDDA: See to the door!

BERTHA, motionless, looks to HEDDA.

The OTHERS, expressionless, also watch HEDDA. They draw in slowly, HEDDA feeling menaced and hemmed in.

Suddenly, the music resumes and they continue dancing.

HEDDA is, once again, forced into the dance.

MISS TESMAN: *(during the dance)* Oh George, it's so wonderful having you home again.

TESMAN: It's wonderful to be back, Auntie Yulie. You know you've been like a mother to me.

AUNT RENA: *(lightly)* And a father.

TESMAN: *(agreeing good-naturedly)* And a father.

MISS TESMAN: You'll always have a soft spot in

your heart for your old aunties, won't you George dear?

TESMAN: *(still dancing)* My, oh my, what a splendid new hat you've bought.

MISS TESMAN: I got it for Hedda's sake.

TESMAN: For Hedda's sake.

MISS TESMAN: So she wouldn't be ashamed of me when we went out walking on the town.

They dance into a close huddle around HEDDA who begins to feel even more claustrophobic and is again prevented from escaping the dance.

BERTHA: *(stops dance, begins imitating her mistress)* Tesman, we simply can't keep that maid on another moment!

MISS TESMAN: *(mock astonishment)* Not keep Bertha?

TESMAN: Why do you say that?

BERTHA: *(acting HEDDA)* Just look at that. She's left her old silly hat lying all over the place.

TESMAN: But . . .

BERTHA: Suppose someone came in and saw it!

TESMAN: But that's Auntie Yulie's hat.

BERTHA: *(mock-embarrassed:— re-examines it, then mock-apologetic)* I didn't look at it very closely, Mrs. Tesman.

The hat is placed on BERTHA's head, then on MISS TESMAN's, RENA's, TESMAN's and finally onto HEDDA which makes everyone shriek with laughter.

HEDDA hurls it in the midst of the group which immediately reactivates the dance. It becomes even more frantic and HEDDA tries even more desperately to escape the OTHERS laughing at her predicament. Suddenly they ALL stop and confront HEDDA with mock outrage.

MISS TESMAN: Please Hedda, don't play dance music tonight. Think of Aunt Rena.

BERTHA: And Eilert!

RENA: And Auntie Yulie!

ALL: *(fiercely)* And everyone else!

The music distorts.

All vanish except HEDDA.

HEDDA: *(alone, to herself)* It's destroying me. All of this is destroying me.

THEA rises, disconsolate and distressed, from her position upstage.

THEA: It'll soon be light.

HEDDA: It's already light.

THEA: Morning. And he still hasn't come home.

HEDDA: It's past seven.

THEA: And still not back.

HEDDA: Not yet.

THEA: No one at all?

HEDDA: And there we were, sitting up all night till four in the morning.

THEA: How I waited for him!

HEDDA: We needn't have bothered.

THEA: Did you sleep at all?

HEDDA: Oh yes. Quite soundly in fact. Didn't you?

THEA: Not a wink. I couldn't Hedda. Not for a moment.

HEDDA: Now, now there's no need to worry. I can imagine quite well what's happened.

THEA: What? Tell me.

HEDDA: It probably got very late at the Judge's and George didn't want to creep in and wake us up in the middle of the night. Probably ashamed to show his face after staying out so late.

THEA: But where can he have gone?

HEDDA: To his aunts probably. They still keep his old room.

THEA: He wouldn't have gone there.

HEDDA: Well perhaps he's stayed behind at the Judge's. Along with Eilert Loevborg who's probably sitting there even now, reading aloud, with vine-leaves in his hair.

THEA: Oh, Hedda, you're just saying that. You know very well it's not so.

HEDDA: You really are a silly little thing, Thea. And you look so tired. Now do as I say. Go straight into my room and lie down for a while.

THEA: No, no, I couldn't sleep now.

HEDDA: Of course you can. I'll call you as soon as he comes in. Now go and lie down.

THEA doesn't move.

Do as I say.

THEA is intimidated out of the room.

HEDDA now approaches BRACK who has been standing silent and glazed.

HEDDA: Tell me. Tell me.

BRACK remains silent.

HEDDA, like a sorceress, stands behind him — repeats 'Tell me' and, on tape, we hear BRACK's voice while BRACK himself stands silent, facing straight out.

BRACK'S VOICE: I had good reason for keeping track of my guests last night. Or I should say, one or two of them. Including, of course, Eilert

Loevborg. They found themselves spirited away to a very lively gathering of a highly sportive nature. I was well aware that Loevborg had received an invitation previously. Of course, he had refused. As you know, he's an entirely reformed character nowadays. But last night at my house, I'm afraid he had an unfortunate lapse. He became very high-spirited. Violently so. And, as a result, yielded to his weaker nature. We mortals, alas, aren't always as high-minded as we would like to be. And so, to make a long story short, he found himself at a private soiree in the home of a certain Madam Diana.

Lights up.

A sumptuous setting — scarlet curtains, a red plush divan; strong whiff of decadence. Operatic aria faint in the background.

MME. DIANA, scantily dressed, lounging on divan, smoking.

BRACK'S VOICE: She was holding what one might call, a select party for some of her girl-friends and their male admirers. She's a singer of sorts, but her main vocation is that of a huntress; a huntresss of men. Eilert Loevborg used to be one of her most ardent admirers. But of course, that was in the bad old days. Nevertheless, Madame Diana welcomed him back with open arms.

Lights fade out on BRACK and HEDDA.

Full up on MME. DIANA's room.

LOEVBORG looking somewhat idealized in HEDDA's eyes, arrives. They regard each other.

*MME. DIANA rises and moves to LOEVBORG.
They kiss. She breaks the kiss and proffers a velvet
box. He looks quizzically to her, takes it and opens it.*

*He looks amused at the contents and smiles at
DIANA, who smiles back. He takes from the velvet
box a crown of golden vine leaves, places them on
his head, and assuming the posture of a greek god,
smiles at DIANA.*

*He then places the crown on her head, and they both
laugh silently.*

*He moves her to the divan and kisses her again.
Begins to fondle her breasts; she, to clutch his
genitals. She then pushes him away. He is surprised
at this rebuff, but DIANA smiles and extends her
leg, inferring that she expects LOEVBORG to
remove her shoes.*

*He kneels before her and does so. Proceeds to
undress her; she, to undress him. Before they are
entirely naked, DIANA kneels down in front of
LOEVBORG as if to give head.*

The operatic aria reaches a climactic point.

Lights flicker for an instant.

*When they are restored, it is HEDDA dressed as
Diana, who is kneeling before LOEVBORG. He
extends his hand and brings her to an upright
position. They kiss tenderly. The kiss grows in heat,
then suddenly HEDDA breaks out of the embrace as
if fearing an intruder. She pushes LOVEBORG out
of the scene and faces downstage-right where
GENERAL GABLER, back to AUDIENCE,
suddenly appears.*

HEDDA, like a guilty child caught by her father, stands clutching clothes to her body. Gradually she drops her covering and with a new assurance, approaches GEN. GABLER. She looks him directly in the eyes and drops down in front of him, her hands visible to the audience around his waist.

The operatic aria, now gentle and lyrical, reaches a climax.

Lights up on BRACK, standing silent.

BRACK: *(on tape, as before, but now more naturalistic)* At least she welcomed him warmly at first, but the tender reception soon got quite rough.

Flicker light of a silent movie.
LOEVBORG dashes in and rudely pulls up DIANA by her shoulders. She knees him in the groin. He clutches himself and falls back over couch.

He accused her, or her friends, of having robbed him. He claimed, among other things, that his wallet had been lifted.

LOEVBERG mimes theft of manuscript. Displays empty folder.

DIANA flips it over her shoulder.

He behaved quite appallingly and in a manner which was decidedly ungallant.

He goes for her. She catches him in a judo hold. He grabs her by the neck and puts her into a hammer-lock.

She mimes screaming for help.

TWO WHORES, flimsily dressed, come to her rescue.

Before long, there was a general melee with both ladies and gentlemen partaking.

DIANA, now freed, blows whistle.

POLICE rush in.

BRACK'S VOICE: Fortunately the police arrived — but that didn't settle matters. They met with quite a stiff resistance.

LOEVBERG gets both POLICEMEN in hammerlocks. They beat him with clubs. He pushes one into ONE WHORE's arms, the OTHER into the OTHER's.

WHORES kiss POLICEMEN to give them renewed valor.

They rush off after their prey again.

He struck one officer over the head and tore the clothes off another.

POLICEMAN loses trousers in scufflle.

He was then requested to accompany them to the station which, reluctantly, he did.

LOEVBERG finally subdued by WHORES is handcuffed by POLICEMEN.

ONE WHORE busts flowerpot over his head which remains framed around it like a hat.

All in all, it turned out a rather costly evening for Master Eilert. Vine-leaves? No. He very decidedly did not have vine-leaves in his hair.

LOEVBERG trundled out by POLICE.

Lights fade out on scene.

Lights up on BRACK with HEDDA.

BRACK: As a friend of the family, I felt it my duty to give you a full account of his nocturnal exploits.

HEDDA: Why?

BRACK: Because I suspect he's intending to hide behind your respectability, Madame Hedda.

HEDDA: What makes you think that?

BRACK: We're neither of us naive, Madame Hedda. You know as well as I that Mrs. Elvstead won't be in any great hurry to return to her husband.

HEDDA: Even if there were anything between them, there are plenty of places they can meet.

BRACK: I think not. From now on every decent house will be closed to Eilert Loevborg — just as before.

DIANA languidly joins HEDDA and begins eyeing BRACK seductively.

HEDDA: And so should mine. Is that what you mean?

BRACK: Let me put it this way. I should find it

disagreeable if this gentleman were to be granted refuge here. If he were to upset . . .

HEDDA: The triangle?

DIANA stretches voluptuously.

BRACK: Precisely. I would feel I had lost a friendly haven.

HEDDA: I see. You want to be the only cock of the walk.

DIANA gazing at BRACK from behind HEDDA's shoulder.

BRACK: You could say that. It means a great deal to me, Madame Hedda, and one fights with every weapon at hand to retain what is dear to one.

As DIANA unwinds from HEDDA in front of him, BRACK takes DIANA into his arms and kisses her hotly.

HEDDA: *(watching academically)* You're quite ruthless aren't you, when you really want something.

BRACK: *(to Diana)* Do you think so?

HEDDA: I'm beginning to. I'm glad you have no hold over me, Judge Brack.

BRACK: Are you, Madame Hedda? Well, you may be right. If I did, who knows what I might do.

HEDDA: That sounds alarmingly like a threat.

BRACK: Perish the thought, Madame Hedda. As you
     well know, triangular relationships only work by
     mutual consent — never by force.

HEDDA: I'm, glad you feel that way too.

*DIANA pulls BRACK onto her and kisses him
brazenly.*

*Suddenly . . . the manuscript is dropped, from the
flies, onto the stage floor.*
*BRACK, DIANA, TESMAN, THEA, MISS
TESMAN and HEDDA appear from all sides and
look towards the dropped object.*

*LOEVBORG makes a leap towards it; MISS
TESMAN kicks it aside to BRACK who picks it up
just as LOEVBORG arrives at his side, and fields it
across to TESMAN.*

*LOEVBORG bears down on TESMAN, but not
before he has thrown it to DIANA, who throws it to
THEA who, about to give it to LOEVBORG, has it
intercepted by BRACK who passes it to MISS
TESMAN, TESMAN, DIANA and finally HEDDA.*

*HEDDA holding the manuscript gestures
EVERYONE off save LOEVBORG and THEA
whom she directs to face each other.*

*Then with a signal from HEDDA, the DIRECTOR,
LOEVBORG, as ACTOR, begins his scene with
THEA as ACTRESS.*

*The following scene is performed by THEA and
LOEVBORG in a highly artificial over-theatrical
manner:*

THEA: Oh Eilert, you've come at last.

LOEVBORG.   Yes — at last — but alas, too late.

THEA: Too late? Too late?

LOEVBORG: Everything is too late now. It's all over,
    Thea. *(looks to HEDDA who cues him to drop his
    head, crestfallen. He does so on cue)* I'm through!

    HEDDA then cues THEA to continue.

THEA: Oh no, no — don't say that!

LOEVBORG: You'll say it yourself, when you've
    heard what I . . .

    HEDDA cues THEA to move away.

THEA: *(moving away)* I won't listen to a word!

HEDDA: *(putting down script, as director)* Would you
    two rather be alone?!

LOEVBORG: *(actor, desperate for direction)* No,
    stay!

THEA: *(....ditto....)* No, stay!

    *HEDDA decides to stay, re-opens script and cues
    THEA.*

HEDDA: 'I don't want to listen . . .'

THEA: I don't want to listen to a word, I tell you.

LOEVBORG: It's not of last night that I wish to
    speak.

THEA: Then what . . .?

LOEVBORG: Just this: Our ways must now part —
          for ever.

THEA: Part?

*HEDDA places THEA's hand on her throat in a
melodramatic gesture to conclude line.*

LOEVBORG: I have no further need of you, Thea.

THEA: You can stand there and say that? No further
          need of me! Surely I can still help you as I did
          formerly. Surely we can continue to work together.
          (beside LOEVBORG)

HEDDA draws LOEVBORG away from THEA

LOEVBORG: My work is done now. For ever!

*HEDDA places his hand on his forehead to suggest
desolation.*

*LOEVBORG shoots HEDDA a look as if to say
'This is too much' but HEDDA insists on the
gesture.*

THEA: Then what shall I do with my life?

HEDDA: *(stridently, giving the reading)* 'Then what
          shall I do with my *life*!'

THEA: *(picking up the reading)* 'Then what shall I do
          with my *life*!'

LOEVBORG: You must try to live now — as if we had never met.

THEA: But I cannot.

LOEVBORG: You must!

THEA: But I cannot!

LOEVBORG: You must!

THEA: But I . . .

LOEVBORG: You must! You must return to your home.

HEDDA draws him away. Then pushes THEA towards him.

THEA: Never, never! Where you are, there too shall I be! I won't be driven away. I must be with you when the book comes out.

Pause as LOEVBORG drops cue, flounders.

HEDDA: *(whispers)* 'Alas, the book!'

LOEVBORG: Alas, the book. Our book. Yours and mine. For that is what it is.

THEA: Yes, yes — I feel that too. And that's why I have the right to be with you when it comes out. I want to see honor and respect showered on you again. And the joy, Eilert — I want to share the joy with you.

HEDDA places THEA alongside LOEVBORG,
their hands clasped, raising his chin high — on a par
with THEA's.

LOEVBORG: *(breaking the pose)* Thea, our book will
never come into the world.

THEA: *(stung)* Ah!

LOEVBORG: *Can* never come into the world!

THEA: Never?

LOEVBORG: Never.

Pause.

THEA: Eilert Loevborg — what have you done with
the manuscript? Answer me!

LOEVBORG: *(turning away)* Oh Thea, don't ask me
that!

THEA: *(directed to pursue him)* Yes, yes. I must
know. I have the right to know. Tell me!

LOEVBORG: The manuscript. Yes. *(pause, he
falters)*

HEDDA mimes next line in vain — eventually she
shows LOEVBORG the line in the script.

LOEVBORG: I've thrown it away. Torn it into a
thousand fragments.

THEA: No, no, no, no, no.

HEDDA slaps her shoulder to stop her going over the top.

Oh my God, my God, torn it into a thousand fragments.

LOEVBORG: I've torn my life into pieces, why not my life's work as well!?

THEA: And you did that — last night?

LOEVBORG: *(dramatizing like mad)* Yes, I tell you. I tore it into a thousand fragments. And scattered them out across the fjord. Far, far out. There, at least, there is clean salt-water. Let them drift in the current and flutter in the wind and finally sink into the deep. Deep, deep into the deep. As shall I, Thea! *(slumps head, exhausted with anguish and acting)*

HEDDA slaps him on the shoulder to denote 'good show'.

LOEVBORG, out of character, smiles, shakes hands with HEDDA.

HEDDA cues THEA.

THEA: *(in a Chekhovian brood)* Do you know Eilert Loevborg, all my life, I shall feel as if you have killed a little child.

LOEVBORG: You're right. It is like murdering a child.

THEA: But how could you? It was my child, too! *Our* child! It's all over now. I must go now, but I know not where. All I can see before me is . . . darkness!

HEDDA snaps her fingers.

There is a blackout.

Lights up

Applause on tape.

All three take curtain calls, THEA and LOEVBORG go off, smiling together.

HEDDA radiating with joy, turns to see TESMAN entering with pram. She turns cold, still and silent.

TESMAN: *(arranging blankets and fussing with pram)* Good heavens, are you up already?

HEDDA: *(distant, subdued)* Yes, I was up early this morning.

TESMAN: I thought you'd be fast asleep. Imagine that.

HEDDA: *(staring into pram, transfixed)* Keep your voice down. Mrs. Elvstead is asleep.

TESMAN: Mrs. Elvstead? Oh dear, has she been here all night?

HEDDA: No one came to escort her back home, did they?

TESMAN: No, no, I suppose they didn't.

HEDDA: Well, was it fun at the Judge's?

TESMAN: Were you worried about me, Hedda?

HEDDA: Not in the least. I only asked whether it had
           been fun.

TESMAN: Oh yes, great fun . . . well at the beginning;
           well, *I* thought so, anyway. Eilert read his book
           aloud. Honestly, Hedda, I can't tell you what a
           book that's going to be. It sounds like one of the
           most remarkable things ever written. You can't
           imagine. *(stops fussing at pram)* I'll confess
           something to you, Hedda. When he'd finished
           reading, a kind of bitter taste came into my mouth.

           *HEDDA is now joined by LOEVBORG who stands
           beside her, arm in arm; the two, as doting parents,
           look down into the pram while TESMAN, oblivious,
           chatters on.*

           I was sitting there squirming with envy because
           Eilert was able to write like that. But isn't it sad,
           Hedda? Despite all his gifts and his talent, he's still
           unsalvageable. What a tragedy.

HEDDA: *(into LOEVBORG's eyes)* You mean that
           he has more courage and less fear than most men.

TESMAN: He simply doesn't know the meaning of
           the word restraint.

HEDDA: *(to LOEVBORG)* And afterwards. What
           happened then?

TESMAN: *(still with pram)* Well, I suppose, thinking
           back to it, you might almost call it an orgy.

HEDDA: *(to LOEVBORG)* Did he have vine-leaves
           in his hair?

TESMAN: No, I don't think so. Didn't see any. But
            he did make a long, rambling speech in honor of
            the woman who had inspired his work.

            *THEA has now taken up a position alongside
            LOEVBORG, as the doting parent, looking down
            into the pram.
            HEDDA has been frozen out.*

HEDDA: Did he mention her name?

TESMAN: No, but I imagine he was referring to Mrs.
            Elvstead. Brack and the rest of us all left at the
            same time. By then, we all needed to get a breath
            of fresh air. And we felt we'd better see Eilert
            home. He was somewhat the worse for wear.

            *LOEVBORG and THEA having toyed with the
            baby in the pram, walk off arm in arm, leaving
            HEDDA with TESMAN.*

            But then this extraordinary thing happened. Well,
            more sad than extraordinary. I'm almost ashamed
            to tell you about it.

HEDDA: Go on.

TESMAN: Well, as we were heading back toward
            town, I fell a bit behind the others, and when I
            hurried to catch up, can you imagine what I found
            lying by the side of the road? Now promise you
            won't say anything to anyone. For Eilert's sake,
            Hedda. I found this. *(produces MS taking it
            from pram. Big pink ribbon on ms)* The whole
            precious, irreplaceable manuscript. He'd just
            dropped it by the roadside without noticing. Can
            you imagine anything so . . .

HEDDA: *(distant)* Why didn't you give it back to him?

TESMAN: In his state? Oh, Hedda, I didn't dare.

HEDDA: Didn't you tell any of the others?

TESMAN: Certainly not. I didn't want to embarrass Eilert. I'll let him sleep it off, get a little nap myself, and then run over and give it back to him.

HEDDA: *(goes for MS)* Let me read it first.

TESMAN: *(withdraws MS)* My dear Hedda, goodness gracious, I couldn't do that. I can just imagine how distracted he'll be when he wakes up and finds it gone. There is no copy. He said so himself. He'll be desperate.

HEDDA: Can't that sort of thing be rewritten?

TESMAN: Not really Hedda. I doubt it. You can't just bring back the inspiration, you know.

HEDDA: No. No, I suppose you can't.

AUNT RENA, dark figure with white, sickly face, is rolled on in a wheelchair by AUNT YULIE.

AUNT RENA: *(in a thin, faint voice)* Georgie . . . Georgie . . .

TESMAN: Auntie Rena . . . Auntie Rena . . .

He sees her in the distance, begins moving towards her, but the closer he comes, the further she is moved away by AUNT YULIE. They both disappear off-

stage, TESMAN still calling her name.

HEDDA stoops down into pram and lifts out its contents — a small twisted, blood-spattered CHILD. She holds it for a moment — then drops it back into the pram.

AUNTIE YULIE and AUNTIE RENA, both dressed in black, like two old crows, appear beside the pram, smile slyly at HEDDA and wheel it away.

HEDDA darts away frightened, and turns into the arms of BRACK — who kisses her hotly. She breaks away, repelled, and runs headlong into LOEVBORG's arms.

BRACK, THEA and TESMAN join in the scene — although LOEVBORG's scene is only with HEDDA.

LOEVBORG: Shall I tell you the truth, Hedda?

TESMAN: For heaven's sake, tell us!

HEDDA: The truth?

BRACK: Eilert Loevborg has been taken to hospital.

THEA: My God!

BRACK: He's dying.

LOEVBORG: Give me your word that you'll never let Thea know about this.

THEA: And we had just quarrelled.

HEDDA: I give you my word.

LOEVBORG: Everything I told her was a lie.

THEA: My God!

HEDDA: About the manuscript?

LOEVBORG: I didn't tear it up. Or throw it into the fjord.

HEDDA: Where is it then?

THEA: What's hapened? Tell me!

LOEVBORG: It's destroyed all the same.

BRACK: Attempted suicide.

THEA: Shot himself!?

LOEVBORG: Thea said that what I had done was like killing a child.

BRACK: This afternoon. In his rooms. Between three and four.

LOEVBORG: But killing a child is not the worst thing a father can do to it.

THEA: But that's impossible.

BRACK: Through the breast.

HEDDA: What would be worse than that?

LOEVBORG: Suppose a father came home one morning.

THEA: But I was there just after six . . .

LOEVBORG: After a night of debauchery . . .

BRACK: It must have been somewhere else then . . .

LOEVBORG: And told the mother of his child: I've been wandering about town all night. To this place and that place. I had our child with me, but now it's lost. Just disappeared.

THEA: *(to herself)* How horrible.

LOEVBORG: God only knows where it is or what's happened to it.

HEDDA: But when all's said and done, it was only a book . . .

THEA: *(stunned)* His mind was unbalanced.

LOEVBORG: Thea's heart and soul were in that book.

THEA: That's why he tore up his manuscript.

LOEVBORG: It was her whole life.

BRACK: Manuscript? Did he tear it up?

THEA: Yes, last night.

HEDDA: I understand.

LOEVBORG: Well then you must also understand there can be no possible future for her and me!

THEA: Then what shall I do with my life?

HEDDA: Where will you go?

LOEVBORG: There's nowhere *to* go. I just want to put an end to it all. The sooner, the better.

HEDDA: Eilert Loevborg, listen to me *(hands him pistol)* Do it beautifully.

LOEVBORG: Beautifully? Wearing a crown of vine-leaves in my hair. The way you used to dream of me in the old days?

HEDDA: I don't have dreams like that any more. But do it beautifully all the same.

LOEVBORG looks down at pistol

You remember it? You've looked down its barrel once before.

LOEVBORG: You should have used it then.

HEDDA: Here you use it now. You must go. And don't come back. But do it beautifully, Eilert Loevborg. Promise me that.

LOEVBORG: Hedda. Hedda Gabler.

They kiss.

He dashes out. HEDDA turns triumphantly to the OTHERS.

HEDDA: *(ecstatic)* Something truly noble, at last!

TESMAN: *(appalled)* For God's sake, Hedda, what are you saying?

HEDDA: I'm saying there is real beauty in what he
    has done.

TESMAN: Beauty? How can you. . . ?

THEA: How can you talk of beauty, Hedda, when
    someone has . . .

HEDDA: Eilert Loevborg has settled all of his
    accounts. He's had the courage to do what he had
    to do.

THEA: He did it because his mind was unbalanced.

TESMAN: Because he was desperate!

HEDDA: Because he had more courage and less fear
    than other men!

*Lights change. The Beautiful Death of EILERT
LOEVBORG.*

*BERTHA walks down the line with tray containing
pistols. Each person takes one.*

ALL line up in military rank.

*LOEVBORG, blindfolded, is brought in by GEN.
GABLER. Placed in isolation opposite the firing-
squad.*

GABLER raises his sword.

ALL OTHERS raise their pistols and take aim.

*LOEVBORG suddenly steps forward, rips blindfold
from his eyes, whips out GABLER's pistol from its*

holster and places barrel against his chest in a heroic gesture.

THEA rushes up to try to stop him.

LOEVBORG shoves her aside, replaces pistol beside breast.

HEDDA approaches, kisses LOEVBORG tenderly, then places the barrel of the pistol in his mouth. Steps back.

There is a thunderous gunshot and, as LOEVBORG falls and THEA screams, a great shower of manuscript pages rains down from the flies above.

Blackout.

In darkness a military drum-roll is heard deafeningly.

Lights up.

A tribunal table is brought on stage.

Around it assemble MRS. TESMAN, THEA, BRACK, the POLICE, the WHORES. At the center of the table, as judge, sits GEN. GABLER.

Before the table, as if in the dock, stands HEDDA. Opposite her, DIANA.

GEN. GABLER gives BRACK a signal. He leaves his position and, as prosecuting attorney, approaches HEDDA, file in hand.

BRACK: *(after consulting his dossier)* Mrs. Hedda.

(suddenly) Where did you put the manuscript?

HEDDA: I no longer have it.

BRACK: No longer have it? What is that supposed to mean?

HEDDA: *(surveys courtroom then after a pause)* I've burned it.

BRACK: Burned it!?

THEA: Burned Eilert Loevborg's manuscript! *(horrified)* Oh no!

TESMAN: Hedda, do you realize what you've done?

THEA: No!

MISS TESMAN: How could you do such a thing!

THEA: No!

TESMAN: What on earth were you thinking of?

THEA: No!

TESMAN: Answer me!

HEDDA: *(looking at George)* I did it for your sake, George.

ALL look at TESMAN.

TESMAN: For my sake?

HEDDA: When you came home . . . and told me how

he'd read his book to you? You admitted you were consumed with jealousy.

BRACK: *(sharply to TESMAN)* Is this true?

TESMAN: Yes, but good God, I never meant it literally.

HEDDA: I couldn't bear the thought that you would be overshadowed by anyone — especially him.

TESMAN: *(touched)* Hedda, is this true? But I never realized that you felt anything like . . .

THEA: *(rising bitterly)* How could you? All my life I shall feel as though you'd killed a little child.

HEDDA: *(making light)* When all's said and done, it was only a book.

GENERAL: *(severe)* Appropriating lost property. Against the law. *(to BRACK)* Proceed.

BRACK: *(consults dossier, then new tack)* Loevborg was here this morning.

HEDDA is silent.

Wasn't he?

HEDDA: Yes.

BRACK: Were you alone with him?

HEDDA: For a little while.

BRACK: You didn't leave the room while he was here?

HEDDA: No.

BRACK: Think again. Are you sure you never left the room?

HEDDA: I might have stepped into the hall — just for a moment.

BRACK: And where was your pistol-case at that time?

HEDDA: It was inside my . . .

BRACK: (*hinting*) Mrs. Hedda . . .

HEDDA: (*beat*) It was lying open on the desk.

BRACK: Have you looked to see if both pistols are still there?

HEDDA: No.

BRACK: You needn't bother. I saw Loevborg's weapon when they found the body. I recognized it at once. From yesterday — and other occasions.

HEDDA: Where is the weapon? (*turns enquiringly to GENERAL*)

GENERAL: With the police.

HEDDA: And what will the police do with it?

GENERAL: Try and trace the owner, of course.

HEDDA: (*to BRACK*) Do you think they will find the owner?

BRACK: *(close to HEDDA — aside)* Not as long as I hold my tongue.

HEDDA: *(quietly)* And if you don't?

BRACK: You could always claim the pistol had been stolen.

HEDDA: I'd rather die.

BRACK: People say that. They never do it. *(to ALL)* And suppose the pistol wasn't stolen? And they trace the rightful owner, what then?

TESMAN: There'll be a scandal, Hedda.

ALL: *(whispered)* A scandal.

Throughout the next dialogue, there is a background of whispering.

BRACK: You'll have to appear in court along with Madame Diana.

MISS TESMAN: She'll have to explain what happened.

TESMAN: Was it an accident?

BRACK: Or was it homicide?

TESMAN: Was he using the pistol just to threaten her?

THEA: Did it go off by accident?

BRACK: Or did she grab the pistol away from him?

THEA: Shoot him and then put it in his pocket?

GENERAL: She might well have done it. I wouldn't put it past her.

BRACK: She's an enterprising lady, Madame Diana.

HEDDA: *(beat)* All of this sordid business has nothing to do with me!

Whispering stops.

BRACK: Eilert Loevborg has meant more to you than you're willing to admit — even to yourself. Is that not true?

HEDDA: I don't have to answer questions like that from you. I only know that Eilert Loevborg has had the courage to live according to his own lights. And now, at last, he's done something noble. Something beauiful. He's had the courage and the will to leave life's feast when he chose.

BRACK: It pains me to say it, Mrs. Hedda, but I'm afraid I must disabuse you of that charming illusion.

HEDDA: Illusion?

BRACK: He didn't shoot himself on purpose.

HEDDA: Not on purpose?

BRACK: The incident didn't occur exactly the way I described it. First of all, it didn't take place at his lodging. Eilert Loevborg was found shot in Madame Diana's boudoir.

HEDDA: *(shoots a look at DIANA, who smiles wanly)*
That's impossible!

BRACK: He went there this afternoon. He was after
something he claimed they'd taken from him.
Talked wildly about a child which had disappeared.
That's where he was discovered. In his breast
pocket, a pistol that had gone off and wounded
him mortally.

HEDDA: In the breast.

BRACK: No, Mrs. Hedda. In the groin.

HEDDA: *(after a pause)* No! No!

*LOEVBORG dishevelled, now in tattered clothes,
with dirty face and blood smeared all over him,
approaches HEDDA.*

LOEVBORG: Why is it that everything I touch turns
squalid and ludicrous? *(falls into HEDDA's arms)*

*HEDDA catches him involuntarily then steps aside
in disgust and horror as the body falls to the floor.*

BRACK: *(bearing down)* Why did you give Eilert
Loevborg that pistol?

*HEDDA looks to the others who sit stone-faced. She
cracks and begins to cry.*

*GEN. GABLER moves forward and takes her in his
arms.*

GEN. GABLER: The greatest misfortune of life, and
no less so for affecting most of mankind, is that

people spend all their time longing for happiness
without ever attaining it. Hedda is no different
from you or me. She's the kind of woman that marries
a Tesman, but spins endless fantasies over a man
like Eilert Loevborg. She reclines in an armchair,
closes her eyes and visualizes daring adventures.
But before long, all kinds of moral considerations
— some acquired — some innate — interrupt her
thoughts. She is tempted irresistibly but never
dares to take the plunge. She dreams, but
doesn't act.

Men and women never belong to the same society,
you know, whatever the period. Women can't
affect large public issues, important events — so
instead, they cast their influence over the inner
lives of certain individuals. In Hedda, there was a
devil that made her long to influence another
human being. The irony is that once she'd cast her
spell over him, she came to despise him. For her,
life was something of an absurdity that wasn't
worth seeing through to the end.

*The GENERAL returns to his position at the center
of the trial table.*

*HEDDA, realizing a verdict is imminent, turns
suddenly and looks expectantly to the PEOPLE
behind the table.*

THEA: Guilty!

MISS TESMAN: Guilty!

1 WHORE: Guilty!

2 WHORE: Guilty!

AUNT RENA: Guilty!

TESMAN: *(after a beat)* Guilty.

> *HEDDA turns to DIANA who smiles, turns and goes.*

> *BRACK approaches HEDDA and helps her up.*

HEDDA: From now on I'm at your mercy, Judge. You've finally got your hold over me.

BRACK: I assure you dear Hedda. I wouldn't for a moment take advantage of such a situation.

HEDDA: Subjugated to your will, and your whims. Not free. Never again, free *(turns to others)* No, no, I couldn't bear that!

BRACK: Most people resign themselves to the inevitable sooner or later.

> *They all leave taking trial table with them.*

> *TESMAN and THEA suddenly start scrambling all over the stage, picking up every stray page of manuscript they can find.*

THEA: If only it could be pieced together again.

TESMAN: *(picking up pages)* If only it could. I'd give anything . . .

THEA: Perhaps it can, Mr. Tesman. I still have the original notes.

TESMAN: *(examining a page in THEA's hand)* Let

me have a look.

THEA: Oh, they're all muddled up.

TESMAN: *(picks up manuscript-page, reads)* 'Why should I follow the dictates of a social morality that has only another half-generation to live. If a man can be friends with several men, then why not also with several women? A relationship based on cameraderie must be forged between man and woman so that a new spiritual being can emerge. Whatever else a couple may do is . . .' *(looks about)*

THEA: *(finding the continuation)* '. . . is entirely immaterial. That is what society cannot understand. Life is not . . .

TESMAN: *(reading)*'Life is not tragic — only absurd, and for that reason, cannot be borne'. Oh, if we could only sort them out. Perhaps, if we were to work together . . .

THEA: Oh, let's at least try!

TESMAN: We can do it. We *will* do it. *(stooping for a sheet)* I'll dedicate my life to it.

HEDDA: You, George. Your life?

TESMAN: *(as he straightens, he appears transformed)* Yes, all the time I have. My own book will have to wait. Don't you understand, Hedda. I owe this to Eilert's memory. *(close to THEA)* Mrs. Elvstead, you and I will have to collaborate together. There's nothing to be gained brooding over the past. We must approach this task in a positive frame of mind.

THEA: I'll do my best.

TESMAN: We can start by collating these pages. Where shall we sit? *(sexually excited)* Here? *(sees HEDDA)* No, over there would be better. You'll excuse us, won't you, Hedda. Come along, Mrs. Elvstead. *(holds her hand, draws her to side of stage)*

THEA: *(excited)* If only we could manage to do it.

They huddle together.

LOEVBORG: *(above them)* Isn't it strange, Thea? Here you are, sitting with Tesman — just the way you used to sit and work with Eilert Loevborg.

THEA: *(To HEDDA)* Wouldn't it be marvellous if I could inspire your husband too?

MISS TESMAN: That will come — in time.

BERTHA: *(to MISS TESMAN, confidentially)* I never dreamed I'd live to see a match between *her* and little Georgie.

TESMAN: Why don't you move into Auntie Yulie's then we could meet up in the evenings and work there.

MISS TESMAN: *(To TESMAN)* George needs you in the house — close at hand. But what do you think your husband would say when you get back?

THEA: I shall never go back there.

MISS TESMAN: Excellent. Excellent.

TESMAN: *(looking up at THEA)* Isn't she lovely to look at?

MISS TESMAN: Lovely.

BERTHA: Lovely.

TESMAN has whispered to THEA.

THEA: *(To HEDDA)* Imagine. He says I've inspired him.

TESMAN: *(drawing THEA away)* I'm sure Judge Brack will be kind enough to keep you company.

BRACK: *(to HEDDA)* Willingly. Every evening, if you like.

LOEVBORG: *(mournfully)* Hedda. Hedda Gabler.

BRACK: We'll have great fun together — you and I.

LOEVBORG: *(nostalgic)* Imparting secrets long into the night . . .

BRACK: *(intimately to HEDDA)* The only cock of the walk.

TESMAN: You won't mind my not being around, I hope.

BRACK: I'll be delighted.

HEDDA turns slowly to LOEVBORG.

LOEVBORG: *(touching her hair gently)* Do it beautifully, Hedda. Promise me that.

MISS TESMAN: *(bidding her farewell)* For George's sake, Hedda Tesman. God bless you and keep you. *(she kisses HEDDA and turns away).*

In turn, THEA, LOEVBORG and TESMAN also kiss HEDDA and likewise turn away.

They all stand at the edge of the stage and look down, as if into a grave.

MISS TESMAN and BERTHA draw out a piece of black linen, the full length of the stage.

BRACK, from behind, slowly rips it down the center.

MISS TESMAN and BERTHA join the OTHERS downstage, looking down.

MISS TESMAN: She died peacefully.

BERTHA: It was quite beautiful, really.

MISS TESMAN: The end came very calmly.

TESMAN: I must dress her and lay her out as best I can. My head is just going round and round. I can't collect my thoughts.

MISS TESMAN: You mustn't take it like that, George.

TESMAN: What do you mean?

MISS TESMAN: You must be glad in your grief. Glad for everything that's happened. I know I am.

THEA: *(to TESMAN)* It will be lonely for you now.

TESMAN: For the first days, certainly . . . *(then brightening)* but it will soon pass, I'm sure.

He kisses THEA, who responds, as AUNT JULIANA fondly looks on with LOEVBORG.

HEDDA: *(slowly)* I often think there's only one thing that I'm really capable of.

BRACK: And what is that, Hedda?

HEDDA: Boring myself to death. *(laughs)* Now you know. *(continues laughing).*

Laughter rises to a high pitch and is suddenly cut short by a thunderous gunshot.

The stage divides in two — like a split egg — EVERYONE on one side, HEDDA on the other.

GEN. GABLER: *(calling out)* Hedda. Hedda Gabler.

HEDDA: Yes. That used to be my name.

Fade out to black.

Curtain

ENEMY OF THE PEOPLE

A Free Adaptation from Henrik Ibsen

COUNTER-POLEMICS

The central character in *Enemy of the People* as in *Julius Caesar* or *Coriolanus* is the populace. As with all 'central characters', it is essential to determine its motives, attitudes and temperament. If *Enemy of the People* is prevented from being a major work, it is because Ibsen has prejudged this 'central character' and made it one-dimensional. So long as 'the people' react arbitrarily to an author's prejudices and are seen to do so, a play must be ideologically suspect. The same of course applies to *Julius Caesar* and *Coriolanus*.

In the nineteenth century, the notion of a man being 'strongest when he stands alone' could be accepted as a stirring Romantic notion. In our contemporary world of factionalism and power politics, this sentiment is more than suspect, it is demonstrably untrue. From a political standpoint, the man who stands alone is not only not strong, he is thoroughly irrelevant to almost every issue. He doesn't even possess symbolic significance since today it is the media which bestow symbolism and they are controlled by their own power-bloc. The moral implication of his stance may have some interest for journalists and philosophers but in the real world, he is thoroughly ineffective. Indeed, it is only when a man with a radical or nonconformist view begins to acquire supporters that his ideas acquire enough power to combat the received-ideas which gave them birth. In 'the real world' as opposed to Ibsen's fantastically polemical universe, the 'man who stands alone' is usually isolated by society in order for him to be drained of influence and eventually silenced. Isolation is a traditional method by which dangerous men are rendered impotent; the one lesson that the Soviet Union appears to have learned thoroughly. A man like Dr. Stockmann who has been continually battered by Establishment forces does not emerge victorious; more likely he is methodically destroyed.

Enemy of the People is a paen of praise to Individualism. As such, one salutes it. But when its message is related to the corrupted currents of our modern world, it becomes clear that we are living in another day and age and the still, lone voice in the wilderness which articulates 'the ideal' has, at best, only a poetic significance. The reward for committed idealism is not the accumulation of inner strength but a one-way ticket to oblivion. The modern world no longer celebrates 'heroes' — only leaders.

This is not what Henrik Ibsen thought nor instilled into *Enemy of the People* and in approaching the adaptation, one should be aware of the difference. In the play, Dr. Stockmann says at one point. 'The life-span of an average truth is about seventeeen or eighteen years, maybe twenty at most.' That was in 1882. Perhaps, by his own calculations, the germinating idea of *Enemy of the People* is eighty years out of date.

CAST

DOCTOR THOMAS STOCKMANN
MRS. STOCKMANN, his wife
PETRA, his daughter
EILIF, son aged 10
MORTON, son aged 8
MAYOR
MORTON KIIL, grandfather
HOVSTAD, editor
BILLING, reporter
ASLAKSEN, publisher
CAPTAIN HORSTER
1ST CITIZEN
2ND CITIZEN
3RD CITIZEN
4TH CITIZEN
WORKERS
TOWNSPEOPLE
DRUNK

Scene: A Public Hall in which a meeting is shortly to take place.

As the audience enters the theater, they are harangued — in groups — by speakers explaining the dangers to the community of North Sea oil excavations, effluents in the lakes and rivers and other forms of environmental pollution. These speakers, who are soon to take their seats in the auditorium to become the townspeople of the play, try to persuade members of the audience of their viewpoint. There should be at least eighteen such 'disputants' scattered throughout the auditorium — all talking simultaneously.

Meanwhile, on stage, preparations are being made for a public lecture.

Eventually, characters from the play appear and form small huddles on the stage. After DR. STOCKMANN has entered and the lecture is about to begin, these groups, donning their period clothes, file down into the auditorium and take their seats.

1ST CITIZEN: *(to another)* So you're here as well, Lamstead?

2ND CITIZEN: I'm at all the public meetings. Never miss one.

3RD CITIZEN: Brought your whistle, have you?

2ND CITIZEN: Never leave home without it. You've got yours?

3RD CITIZEN: Right here. And old Evensen said he'd be bringing his cowhorn.

2ND CITIZEN: Always prepared. Good old Evensen.

4TH CITIZEN: What's it all about? What's happening tonight?

2ND CITIZEN: It's Dr. Stockman. He's going to have a go at the Mayor.

4TH CITIZEN: But the Mayor is his brother, isn't he?

1ST CITIZEN: Makes no difference to him. You can't scare Thomas Stockmann.

3RD CITIZEN: According to the *People's Tribune,* he's in the wrong.

2ND CITIZEN: He must be. They wouldn't rent him a room either at the Civic Club or the Householders Association.

1ST CITIZEN: He couldn't even get a meeting room at the Baths.

2ND CITIZEN: Bloody certain he wouldn't get one there.

1ST CITIZEN: Whose side are we supposed to be on in all this business?

4TH CITIZEN: Just keep your eye on Aslaksen and do the same as he does. That's what I'm going to do.

BILLING *enters from side of the stage with portfolio under his arm pushing his way through the crowd towards his seat on the side.*

BILLING: Excuse me please, gentlemen. Can I get through please? I'm covering this for the *People's Tribune.* Thank you very much.

WORKER: Who does he think he is?

2ND WORKER: It's Billing that works for Aslaksen's paper.

CAPTAIN HORSTER *enters along with* MRS. STOCKMANN, PETRA, EILIF *and* MORTON.

CAPTAIN HORSTER: I think it might be best if you sit here. Then you can slip out easily if anything should happen.

MRS. STOCKMANN: Do you think there might be trouble then?

CAPTAIN HORSTER: You never can tell with a crowd like this. Anyway just sit down and don't worry.

MRS. STOCKMANN: It was so kind of you to offer my husband the use of this hall.

CAPTAIN HORSTER: Well, it didn't seem like anyone else was going to let him have a place.

PETRA: It was a very brave thing to do, Captain Horster.

CAPTAIN HORSTER: Oh, I don't think it took very much courage.

HOVSTAD and ASLAKSEN come through the crowd towards the platform. ASLAKSEN speaks to CAPTAIN HORSTER.

ASLAKSEN: Hasn't the Doctor arrived yet?

CAPTAIN HORSTER: He's waiting inside.

HOVSTAD: *(to BILLING)*. Look, here comes the Mayor.

BILLING: By God, he's actually come after all!

The MAYOR moves towards CAPTAIN HORSTER and the STOCKMANN family, shaking hands all round. A small group of citizens move to greet him. He gives them a very warm handshake and smiles jovially to the group. He is dressed in a very dapper frock-coat and red waistcoat and looks both formal and debonair. As he is taken up in conversation with MRS. STOCKMANN, DR. STOCKMANN enters from door, stage left — somewhat furtive and selfconscious. The group clears a path for him and immediately begins murmuring. DR. STOCKMANN moves towards his wife and family engaging them in subdued conversation.

DR. STOCKMANN: Are you alright Katherine?

MRS. STOCKMANN: I'm alright. *(quietly)*. Now promise me you won't lose your temper, Thomas.

DR. STOCKMANN: Don't worry. I know how to control myself. *(looks at his watch)*. It's a quarter past. I'd better begin.

Takes out his manuscript and begins to move towards

the lectern. The general murmur of the crowd very gradually dies down as everyone gets seated. Just before DR. STOCKMANN is about to commence ASLAKSEN, sitting at the side, speaks.

ASLAKSEN: Surely we should elect a chairman before anything else?

DR. STOCKMANN: A chairman? There's no need for that.

The crowd begins to murmur assent at this suggestion and eventually concurs vocally.

CITIZENS: *(shouting).* A chairman! A chairman! Let's have a chairman!

MAYOR: I agree it would certainly be correct procedure to elect a chairman.

DR. STOCKMANN: But I have called this meeting in order to deliver a lecture.

MAYOR: That may well be, but a lecture by the Public Health Officer might possibly give rise to strong differences of opinion.

SEVERAL VOICES FROM THE CROWD: A chairman! Let's have a chairman!

HOVSTAD: The general concensus seems to be in favor of electing a chairman.

DR. STOCKMANN: Very well then, let the general concensus have its way.

ASLAKSEN: Perhaps the Mayor would be so kind as

to assume that function?

THE CROWD enthusiastically agrees.

MAYOR: Thank you. Thank you, friends. But I feel I
must decline the honor for several reasons which
I am sure you will appreciate. However, we are
fortunate to have amongst us a man who I think
can admirably fill that position, I refer to the
chairman of the Householders Association, and
erstwhile printer, Mr. Aslaksen.

CROWD: Yes, yes good old Aslaksen! Hurrah for
Aslaksen!

*DR. STOCKMANN picks up his manuscript and
takes a few steps back. ASLAKSEN, egged on by
THE CROWD, moves to behind the lectern, very
self-effacing.*

ASLAKSEN: Since it appears to be the unanimous
wish of the meeting that I should officiate, I can
hardly refuse.

*Loud applause and cheering from THE CROWD for
ASLAKSEN.*

BILLING: *(writing).* 'Mr. Aslaksen was elected
chairman by general acclamation . . .'

ASLAKSEN: *(suddenly arrogant).* Now since I have
been elected chairman, I should like to be permitted
to say a few brief words. As you all know, I am a
quiet and peaceloving man and a firm believer in
moderate discretion or, as one might say, discreet
moderation. Everyone who knows me, knows that.

CROWD: Yes! That's right! Good old Aslaksen! Hurray!

ASLAKSEN: For I have learnt in the hard school of life that moderation is the one virtue by which a citizen can reveal himself at his best . . .

MAYOR: Hear, hear!

ASLAKSEN: . . . and that moderation, coupled with discretion, can always be counted upon to serve the community best. I would therefore urge the speaker who has called this meeting tonight, to endeavor to keep himself within the bounds of moderation, and above all, to maintain a certain degree of temperance.

DRUNK: *(in back of hall)* Temerance, yes, here's to the bloody temperance society. Three cheers!
Hip Hip Hurray!
Hip Hip Hurray!
Hip Hip Hurray!

THE CROWD quiets down the drunk with various cries of 'Shut him up', 'Get that drunk out of here', 'Kick him out' etc. After THE DRUNK has been removed and the noise subsides, DR. STOCKMANN again approaches the lectern. Before he gets there, ASLAKSEN returns to his former position, stepping immediately in front of DR. STOCKMANN.

ASLAKSEN: Please, gentlemen, no more interruptions. Does anyone wish to say anything before I . . .

MAYOR: Mr. Chairman . . .

ASLAKSEN: His Worship, the Mayor.

MAYOR: Ladies and gentlemen, in view of my close
personal ties to the Medical Officer of the Public
Baths, I should have preferred not be say anything
this evening, but my position as chairman of the
Municipal Baths Committee and my natural
concern for the vital interests of our town compel
me, at this stage, to move a resolution. I think I am
right in saying that no one present here tonight
would like to see unreliable and exaggerated
accounts of the sanitary conditions of the Baths,
and of the town itself, circulated abroad . . .

CROWD: No, no! Certainly not!
Boo! Never!

MAYOR: Therefore, I move that this meeting
disallows the Public Health Officer of the Baths
from publicly delivering his proposed lecture on
this subject.

DR. STOCKMANN: (*flaring up*) Disallows! What in
Hell's name . . .

MRS. STOCKMANN: (*coughing*) Aahem . . . Aahem.

DR. STOCKMANN: (*collecting himself*). Well, go on
then . . .

MAYOR: In my statement to the *People's Tribune*
two days ago, I tried to lay the essential facts before
the public in such a way that every fair-minded
citizen could form his own opinion. I pointed out
in this letter that the Public Health Officer's
proposals, apart from amounting to a vote of no
confidence in the leading citizens of this town,

would saddle the rate payers with an unnecessary expenditure of at least one hundred thousand crowns.

CROWD hisses, boos, catcalls and makes general sounds of disapproval.

ASLAKSEN: *(ringing his bell)* Order! Order, please! I should like wholeheartedly to second the Mayor's motion. It is also my opinion, and I feel I must say this, that the doctor's allegations have an ulterior motive. He speaks of the Baths but what he is really talking about is revolution. What he really wants is to see the administration of our town in other hands. Now, no one doubts the Doctor's sincerity or the honesty of his intentions. No one can be in two minds about that. As for myself, I too am in favor of government by the people, so long as the bill isn't borne by the tax payers, but in this case, that's exactly what would happen! And that's why I'll be damned — if you'll pardon my saying so — if I will support Dr. Stockmann in this matter. There is such a thing as paying too high a price even for gold — that's my opinion, anyway.

THE CROWD applauds and approves from all sides.

HOVSTAD: *(rising)* If you will permit Mr. Chairman, I feel that I too, must declare my position in this matter. At first, Doctor Stockmann's protest won considerable sympathy and I myself supported his views as impartially as I could, but before long it became abundantly clear that we had been misled by a complete misrepresentation of the facts . . .

DR. STOCKMANN: Misrepresentation!

HOVSTAD: Well then, an incomplete view of the situation. This was clearly confirmed by His Worship the Mayor's letter the other day! I don't expect that anyone here tonight would in any way question my own liberal convictions. The attitude of the *People's Tribune* on all pressing political issues is well known to everyone in this hall but I have learnt from long experience that, in the case of delicate local issues, a newspaper must proceed with a certain caution and be guided by men of good faith, sound judgement and experience.

ASLAKSEN: Hear, hear. I entirely agree with the speaker.

HOVSTAD: And in the matter before us, it has become increasingly clear over the last two days, that Doctor Stockmann has the majority of the right-thinking public against him and, ladies and gentlemen, I would ask you this: what is the first and foremost duty of an editor? Is it not to act judiciously and in the best interests of his readers? Has he not been given — as it were — a mandate to work tirelessly on behalf of those people that represent his public? Or am I mistaken in all this?

CROWD: Hear, hear! Hear, hear! Hovstad's right! Bravo! Bravo! *(whistles, etc.)*

HOVSTAD: It has cost me a great deal to have to break with a man in whose house I have been a frequent guest; a man who up till now enjoyed the wholehearted respect and goodwill of his fellow citizens; a man whose only, or at least, most serious fault is that he is swayed rather too much by his heart than by his head.

SEVERAL VOICES FROM THE CROWD: Hear, hear! That's true! Good old Stockmann! Three cheers for Doctor Stockmann!

HOVSTAD: But my duty to the public at large compelled me to take that step and there is another consideration which forces me to oppose him in this matter and if possible, to stop him before he plunges our entire community into disaster, and that is consideration for his family. . .

DR. STOCKMANN: Stick to the issue. The water supply — the sewers.

HOVSTAD: . . . consideration I say, for his wife and his unprovided children.

MORTON: *(turning to MRS. STOCKMANN)* Does he mean us, mother?

MRS. STOCKMANN: Hush!

ASLAKSEN: I will now put His Worship the Mayor's motion to the vote.

DR. STOCKMANN: There's no need. I have no intention of saying anything tonight about the filth of the Baths. I have something quite different to say here tonight.

DRUNK: *(in back of hall)*. I pay my taxes. I've got a right to have my say. It's my firm, unshakeable and unutterable opinion that . . .

SEVERAL VOICES FROM THE CROWD: Shut him up! Quiet over there! Get him out of here! He's drunk! Throw him out!

THE DRUNK is removed. The public gradually subsides.

DR. STOCKMANN: May I have the floor?

ASLAKSEN: *(ringing bell)* Doctor Stockmann has the floor.

Pause.

DR. STOCKMANN: A few days ago if anyone had tried to muzzle me, as has been done here tonight, I'd have fought tooth and nail for my rights. But now all that doesn't matter because I have other, far more important things to speak about.

MORTON KIIL enters from the side and conspicuously moves across the stage to his seat beside the STOCKMANN family. Dr. STOCKMANN continues.

DR. STOCKMANN: I've been thinking a great deal these past few days; about so many things; pondering so many different problems that it made my head spin . . .

MAYOR: *(coughs)* Aahem . . . Aahem.

DR. STOCKMANN: . . . but eventually my head cleared and I began to see things in a new perspective, and that's why I'm standing here tonight because, ladies and gentlemen, I've a revelation to make. I've made a discovery. Something much more far-reaching than the fact that our water supply is polluted and our health resort is riddled with pestilence.

SEVERAL VOICES FROM THE CROWD:
(*scattered, shouting*) Not the Baths! Keep the Baths out of it! Don't mention the Baths! We won't listen! (*catcalls, hisses etc*)

DR. STOCKMANN: The discovery that I have made over these past few days is that it is our entire moral life that is polluted, that the whole of our social conduct is itself founded upon a cesspit of lies!

Crowd reacts angrily.

Cut to side stage. DOCTOR STOCKMANN's living room.

PETRA: (*with letter*) The postman gave it to me as I was going out . . .

DR. STOCKMANN: (*grabbing it*) And you only give it to me now!

PETRA: I didn't have the time to run up again.

DR. STOCKMANN: (*opening the letter and reading it quickly*) Yes, this is it.

MRS. STOCKMANN: Is that what you've been waiting for so anxiously, Thomas?

DR. STOCKMANN: Exactly. This news will shake up the town, I can tell you.

BILLING: News?

MRS. STOCKMANN: What sort of news?

DR. STOCKMANN: A discovery, Katherine, a great discovery!

HOVSTAD: Really?

MRS. STOCKMANN: Of yours?

DR. STOCKMANN: Yes, of mine *(pacing furiously)*. Now let them call me a crank — full of wild ideas. They'll have to sit up and take notice now whether they like it or not.

PETRA: For Heaven's sake, Father, what is it?

DR. STOCKMANN: It just goes to show you how blithely we all go around making judgements — blind as moles . . .

HOVSTAD: What are you referring to Doctor?

DR. STOCKMANN: It's generally supposed, is it not, that our town is one of the healthiest places in the country?

HOVSTAD: Yes.

DR. STOCKMANN: An exceptionally healthy place in fact? A place which deserves to be recommended in the most glowing terms, both for invalids and holiday makers alike?

MRS. STOCKMANN: Yes, but my dear Thomas —

DR. STOCKMANN: And we've all praised it to the skies, have we not? I myself have written about it in the *People's Tribune* — pamphlets, brochures . . .

HOVSTAD: Yes, yes, but so what?

DR. STOCKMANN: These Baths which we've called 'the mainstay of our community', 'the nerve center of the town' and God knows what else . . .

BILLING: 'The pulsing heart of our fair city' I remember calling them once in an after dinner speech!

DR. STOCKMANN: Well, do you know what they actually are? These marvelous, palatial, exceptional Baths that have cost so many thousands — do you know what they actually are?

HOVSTAD: What are they then?

DR. STOCKMANN: Nothing but a bloody cesspit!

PETRA: The Baths?

MRS. STOCKMANN: *(simultaneously)* Our Baths —

HOVSTAD: *(simultaneously)* But, Doctor! —

BILLING: Incredible! Absolutely incredible!

DR. STOCKMANN: These Baths are a whited sepulchre and a poisoned one at that, a menace, a positive menace to the health of everyone who uses them. All that filth up in Molledal, all that foul pollution from the tanneries has infected the water in the pipes that feed the pump room and it is this same poisonous muck that's even seeping out onto the beach —

BILLING: Where the seabaths are?

DR. STOCKMANN: Precisely there.

HOVSTAD: But how can you be certain of all this,
          Doctor?

DR. STOCKMANN: Last year there were a number
          of inexplicable cases of illness among the bathers
          — typhoid and gastric complaints.

MRS. STOCKMANN: Yes, so there were.

DR. STOCKMANN: At the time we thought the
          visitors had brought the infections with them, but
          later during the winter I began to have second
          thoughts. So I decided to analyze the water as
          closely as possible.

MRS. STOCKMANN: So that's what you've been so
          busy with.

DR. STOCKMANN: Yes, but of course I lacked the
          necessary laboratory equipment, so I had the
          samples of both the drinking water and the seawater
          sent to the University to have an accurate analysis
          done by a chemist.

HOVSTAD: And that's what's in that letter you've
          got there!

DR. STOCKMANN: (exhibiting letter) Yes it's all
          there! It proves conclusively the presence of
          putrefying organic matter in the water. It's alive
          with organisms, which means it's harmful to one's
          health whether taken internally or externally.

MRS. STOCKMANN: What a blessing you discovered
          it in time.

DR. STOCKMANN: You may well say that, Katherine.

BILLING: And what do you intend to do now, Doctor?

DR. STOCKMANN: Remedy the situation at once, of course.

BILLING: And you think that can be done?

DR. STOCKMANN: Can be? It must be done. Otherwise the Baths will be completely unusable and all our work ruined. But don't worry, I've a pretty fair idea as to what has to be done.

MRS. STOCKMANN: And to think, Thomas, you've kept all this a secret.

DR. STOCKMANN: Would you rather I ran out into the streets and blabbed it all over the place before I was certain? I'm not that big a fool.

PETRA: Still, you might have told *us*.

DR. STOCKMANN: I couldn't tell a single living soul. But tomorrow, on your way to school, you can pop into the Old Badger's . . .

MRS. STOCKMANN: *(disapprovingly)* Oh, Thomas!

DR. STOCKMANN: Oh well, to Grandfather's then. It'll be a nice surprise for the old boy. He's always saying I'm round the bend and he's not the only one. Don't think I haven't heard. But now, all these good people, they'll have another think coming. *(walks about delightedly)* What a ruckus there'll be in town! Can you just imagine it! All the water pipes, the whole system will have to be relaid!

HOVSTAD: The whole system?

DR. STOCKMANN: Naturally. The intake is too low. It'll all have to be put much higher up.

PETRA: So, you were right after all?

DR. STOCKMANN: Yes. Do you remember, Petra? I put it all in a letter to the Town Clerk when they began to lay the foundations, but no one took a blind bit of notice then. Well, they'll sit up and take notice now, I can tell you. *(takes out pages from inside pocket)* Look at this. I've prepared a full and detailed report for the Baths Committee. In fact, it's been lying on my desk for over a week now, just waiting for this to come. *(flourishes letter)* Now they're going to get it good and hard. And for good measure, I'll send this report along with it. Katherine, get me something to wrap it in — any old thing will do, and give it to . . . to . . . give it to . . . what the Devil is she called? The maid! And tell her to take it down to the Mayor's office at once.

MRS. STOCKMANN rushes out.

PETRA: What do you think Uncle Peter will say?

DR. STOCKMANN: What can he say? He can only be grateful that all this has come to light.

HOVSTAD: If you've no objection Doctor, I should like to insert a small paragraph about this in the next issue of the *Tribune*.

DR. STOCKMANN: Not at all. In fact, I should be quite grateful if you did.

HOVSTAD: Only I really think that the sooner the
    public know about this, the better.

DR. STOCKMANN: Yes, yes. Of course.

MRS. STOCKMANN re-enters.

MRS. STOCKMANN: She's gone off with it.

BILLING: By God, Doctor, you'll be the First Citizen
    of the town when this gets out. *(claps him on the
    shoulder, as does HOVSTAD)*

DR. STOCKMANN: *(turning to public)* A cesspit of
    lies!

CUT back to public meeting.

VOICES FROM THE CROWD: *(low murmur)*
    What's that? What did he say?

MAYOR: These are preposterous insinuations.

ASLAKSEN: *(ringing bell)* I must ask the speaker to
    moderate his language.

DR. STOCKMANN: I have loved this town as deeply
    as any man can love the place where he was born
    and spent his childhood days. I was only a boy
    when I left it, and distance, absence, nostalgia seems
    to cast a warm glow for me over both the town and
    its people. *(Some applause and approving cries are
    heard)* Then, for years I was buried up north, stuck
    in a dreadful backwater — my patients scattered
    thoughout a bleak and stony terrain — in some
    cases indistinguishable from the hovels in which

they lived. I often thought those poor, starving creatures would have been better off with a vet rather than a doctor.

Discontented murmurs are heard among the audience.

BILLING: By God, now I've heard everything.

HOVSTAD: That is a filthy slander against decent working people.

DR. STOCKMANN: Just a minute! I don't think anyone here could accuse me of forgetting my birth place while I was away. I was like an eider-duck brooding on her nest and what I hatched out was a plan for these Baths. *(Applause and protests intermingled)* Then finally, fate smiled upon me and I was able to return and when I did so, I had only one ambition; a burning desire to work with all my heart for the welfare of my home and community.

MAYOR: *(facing straight out)* You certainly have a peculiar way of doing it.

DR. STOCKMANN: I went around wallowing in my new found happiness but yesterday morning — no, it was the night before actually — my eyes were opened wide and the first sight I saw was the collossal stupidity of the municipal authorities.

Uproar, shouts and laughter. MRS STOCKMANN coughs frantically.

MAYOR: Mr. Chairman —

ASLAKSEN: *(ringing bell)* Doctor, as chairman . . .

DR. STOCKMANN: Let's not quibble about words Mr. Aslaksen. What I mean is that I suddenly realized what a deplorable state we had fallen into because of our illustrious civic leaders. I've had my fill of them — enough to last me the rest of my life. They're like goats rooting around in a garden. They ruin everything they touch. They're in your way wherever you turn. I'd like to see the whole lot of them exterminated like any other vermin . . .

General uproar and protests.

MAYOR: Mr. Chairman, are such statements to be allowed to pass without censure?

ASLAKSEN: *(hand on bell)* Doctor!

DR. STOCKMANN: The only thing that really surprises me is why I hadn't seen through these illustrious gentlemen before. I'd had a perfect example right in front of my eyes all the time. My brother Peter; a model of prejudice and procrastination.

Laughter, confusion, whistling etc as MAYOR moves to side stage.

Cut to side stage. DR. STOCKMANN's living room. The MAYOR holds DR. STOCKMANN's manuscript in his hands.

MAYOR: Do you intend to place this document before the Baths Committee as an official report?

DR. STOCKMANN: Of course! Something must be done about it, and quickly.

MAYOR: As usual, you haven't been able to resist your flamboyant means of expression. This is a rather remarkable report. You say, among other things, that what we're offering our visitors is a course of slow poison.

DR. STOCKMANN: Well, how else could you describe it, Peter? The water in the Baths is unfit for human consumption and equally unfit to bathe in, and this is what we offer to the poor invalids who come here in good faith and pay through the nose to be cured.

MAYOR: And your conclusion is that we must not only build a sewer to carry off the alleged impurities from Molledal, but that all the water pipes must be relaid as well!

Lights up on MORTON KIIL who is standing beside DOCTOR STOCKMAN.

KIIL: Is it true? All this nonsense about the water works!

DR. STOCKMANN: Of course it's true.

KIIL: What was it now? Some animals or something had got into the water pipes?

DR. STOCKMANN: Bacteria.

KIIL: Quite a lot, according to Petra. A whole boatload in fact.

DR. STOCKMANN: Millions probably.

KIIL: And no one can see them!

DR. STOCKMANN: Of course one can't see them!

KIIL: I'll be dammed if this isn't the barmiest thing
I've heard from you yet.

DR. STOCKMANN: What do you mean?

KIIL: You'll never get the Mayor to believe something
like that. Do you think he's that daft?

DR. STOCKMANN: I hope the whole town will be
that daft.

KIIL: The whole town! I suppose anything is possible.
It would serve them right. They chucked me off
the Council — drove me out like a dog, they did,
but they'll pay for it now. You make jackasses out
of them, Stockmann. You're the one to do it, my
boy. And if you can rub the Mayor's nose in it, I'll
donate a hundred crowns to the poor without
blinking an eye. Yes, you're just the sort of clown
who can do it, Stockmann.

DR. STOCKMANN: But it's true.

KIIL: Pull out all the stops, my boy. Do your
damnedest. I'll see you're taken care of. By God, I
will.

Lights out on MORTON KIIL. DOCTOR

*STOCKMANN speaks, returning to scene with
MAYOR.*

DR. STOCKMANN: I see no other way out. Maybe
you can.

MAYOR: I made an excuse to call on the local engineer
this morning. I brought up some of the measures
you've mentioned in this report as things we might
consider sometime in the future . . .

DR. STOCKMANN: In the future!

MAYOR: He just laughed at what he took to be my
extravagant ideas. Have you, by any chance,
stopped to consider what your proposed alterations
would cost? According to his estimates I would
place it somewhere between forty and fifty thousand
crowns.

DR. STOCKMANN: Really? As much as that?

MAYOR: Yes, as much as that. And that's not all.
The job would take a minimum of two years.

DR. STOCKMANN: Two years. Really, two whole
years?

MAYOR: At the minimum. And what are we supposed
to do with the Baths in the meantime? Shut them
up? Well, we'd have to. You don't suppose anyone
would ever come near the place once it got round
there was something wrong with the water.

DR. STOCKMANN: But Peter, there *is!*

MAYOR: We're not the only resort town along this

coast, you know. As soon as word gets out, the others wouldn't lose a second and they'd go to any length to lure the tourists to themselves. Don't mistake that. And then where would we be? We'd probably have to shut down the Baths for good, abandon the whole undertaking, make it a complete write-off and all because of you. You would have ruined your own town.

DR. STOCKMANN: I? . . . ruined? . . .

MAYOR: It's only as a health resort — a spa, that this town has any future worth mentioning. Surely you can see that as well as anyone else?

DR. STOCKMANN: Then what do you propose?

MAYOR: I'm in no way convinced that the condition of the Baths is anything like as serious as you make out.

DR. STOCKMANN: I tell you that if anything, it's worse! Or at any rate, it will be in the summer when the hot weather sets in.

MAYOR: As I have said, I think the report is rather exaggerated. In any case, the existing water system at the Baths is a fact and must be accepted as such. However, that isn't to say that at a later date, the committee might not be prepared — subject to the necessary finance being available, of course — to consider the possibility of making certain modifications . . .

DR. STOCKMANN: And do you think I would allow myself to be a party to such a fraud?

MAYOR: Fraud?

DR. STOCKMANN: Yes, fraud! A misrepresentation
   of the facts, a lie, a crime — not only against the
   public but against the whole notion of civilized
   society.

MAYOR: As I have already said, I'm in no way
   convinced that there is actually any imminent
   danger . . .

DR. STOCKMANN: Oh yes you are! You can't not
   be convinced! You just refuse to admit it and that's
   because it was you who got the Baths and the water
   pipes built on their present site. It was you who is
   responsible for that original blunder and you're
   afraid to admit it! Don't you think I can see right
   through you?

MAYOR: And even if that were true; if I did show a
   little concern for my reputation, it's also for the
   good of the town! Without moral authority I
   shouldn't be able to conduct affairs in the best
   interests of the public. For that reason, and for
   others I could mention, it is imperative that your
   report is not placed before the committee. In the
   public interest, it must be withheld! Later on, I
   shall tactfully bring up the matter for discussion
   and we'll do the best we can without any fuss or
   publicity. But for the present, not a word of this
   matter must leak out to the public.

DR. STOCKMANN: Well, that can't be prevented,
   my dear Peter.

MAYOR: It shall and must be prevented.

DR. STOCKMANN: It can't be I tell you — too many people already know about it.

MAYOR: Know about it? Who? What people? *(beat)* Surely not those fellows on the *People's Tribune.*

DR. STOCKMANN: Yes, the free and independent press of this town will see that you do your duty, whether you want to or not.

MAYOR: *(after a pause)* You know Thomas, you are a thoroughly incorrigible hothead, I don't suppose it has occurred to you that this may well have serious consequences for you?

DR. STOCKMANN: Serious consequences for me?

MAYOR: Yes, and your family.

DR. STOCKMANN: Just what are you driving at?

MAYOR: Thomas, I think I'm right in saying that I've always been a good brother to you. I've always tried to lend you a helping hand and do what I could for you . . .

DR. STOCKMANN: You have, and I am grateful for it.

MAYOR: You needn't be. I did all that as much for my own sake as for yours. It's rather painful for a public servant to have his nearest relative constantly behaving irresponsibly; putting his foot in it time after time.

DR. STOCKMANN: And that's what I do, is it?

MAYOR: Unfortunately, you do. And without even
            knowing it. No sooner do you get some hare-brained
            idea than you immediately dash off an article or a
            pamphlet on the subject.

DR. STOCKMANN: Isn't it one's duty to
            communicate with the public when one has a new
            idea that concerns them?

MAYOR: The public doesn't want any new ideas.
            The public is better off with the old established
            ideas it's used to.

DR. STOCKMANN: And you have the gall to say
            that — straight out.

MAYOR: Yes, Thomas, for once I'm going to speak
            to you bluntly. I've usually tried to avoid that
            because I know how touchy you are, but it's about
            time you heard some home truths. You have no
            idea of the harm you do to yourself because of your
            impetuosity. Always complaining to the authorities
            and criticizing the government, telling them they
            don't know their own business, shouting them
            down and then, when they pay you no mind,
            insisting you've been slighted and treated as a
            crank. You're an impossible man to work with!
            You've no consideration whatsoever, for anyone or
            anything. You seem to overlook the fact that you
            have me, and only me, to thank for your
            appointment as medical officer to the Baths . . .

DR. STOCKMANN: I was entitled to that post. I was
            the first person to see that this town could become
            a flourishing bathing resort.

MAYOR: No one denies that, but it wasn't the right

time for it then — though you weren't to know
that in your remote little world up north — but as
soon as the opportune moment arrived, I and
others took up the matter and . . .

DR. STOCKMANN: Made a complete mess of it.
Completely discarded my original plan and ruined
the whole thing! We can see now how brilliant you
and your colleagues were!

MAYOR: You're just looking for a pretext for another
fight — attacking your superiors, it's an old habit
of yours! You can't bear authority. You never
could. However, I hope I've made it plain to you
just how much is at stake for the town and for
myself too, and I am not prepared to compromise
in my demand.

DR. STOCKMANN: What demand?

MAYOR: As you've been indiscreet enough to discuss
this matter with outsiders — which should in fact
have been treated as highly confidential information
— it is obviously too late to hush things up. All
kinds of rumors will have spread far and wide and
the more malicious elements amongst us will do all
they can to feed those rumors. Therefore, it is
esential for you to issue a public denial.

DR. STOCKMANN: I don't understand you.

MAYOR: That on further investigation, you have
convinced yourself that the subject isn't nearly as
critical as you had first supposed.

DR. STOCKMANN: And you expect me to do that,
do you?

MAYOR: And furthermore, you will publicly express
            your confidence that the Board of Directors will do
            all that may be necessary to remedy any possible
            defects.

DR. STOCKMANN: I am telling you, Peter, it is my
            clear and absolute personal conviction that . . .

MAYOR: As a public servant you've no right to any
            personal convictions.

DR. STOCKMANN: *(dumbfounded)* No right to . .

MAYOR: Not in your official capacity. As a private
            individual, of course that's quite another matter,
            but as a subordinate official employed by the Baths,
            you've no right to express a conviction that is in
            conflict with that of your superiors.

DR. STOCKMANN: This is too much. I, a doctor, a
            man of science, have no right to . . . !

AYOR: This is not a purely scientific matter. It is
            much more complicated than that. There's not
            only a financial aspect, but a technical one as well.

DR. STOCKMANN: I don't give a damn about any
            of that! Nothing's going to stop me from speaking
            my mind on any subject under the sun!

MAYOR: As long as it has nothing to do with the
            Baths. That, surely you can see, we must forbid.

DR. STOCKMANN: *(shouting)* Forbid! You have
            the gall to forbid . . .

MAYOR: Yes forbid, Thomas. I, as Chairman of the

Committee and your immediate superior, forbid it, and if I forbid it, you have to obey!

DR. STOCKMANN: *(controlling himself)* Peter, if you weren't my brother . . .

PETRA dashes in, followed by MRS. STOCKMANN.

PETRA: Don't stand for it, Father. Don't stand for it!

MRS. STOCKMANN: *(trying to hold her)* Petra, Petra!

MAYOR: So now we've taken to eavesdropping as well.

MRS. STOCKMANN: The walls are so thin we couldn't help but . . .

PETRA: Yes, I was listening!

MAYOR: Well, I'm not altogether sorry.

DR. STOCKMANN: Well, go on: you were talking about forbidding and obeying?

MAYOR: You forced me to adopt that tone.

DR. STOCKMANN: So I'm to make a public statement declaring that I'm a liar, is that it?

MAYOR: We consider it essential that you issue a public statement along the lines I have indicated.

DR. STOCKMANN: And if I don't obey?

MAYOR: Then we shall have to issue a statement ourselves to reassure the public.

DR. STOCKMANN: Very well, I can write too, you know! I shall prove quite conclusively that I am right and you are wrong. And what will you do then?

MAYOR: Then I shall be unable to prevent your dismissal.

DR. STOCKMANN: What!

PETRA: Father!

MRS. STOCKMANN: Dismissal!

MAYOR: Your dismissal as medical officer to the Baths. I shall have no alternative but to propose that you are given instant notice and have no further connection whatsoever with the Baths.

DR. STOCKMANN: And you would dare to do that?

MAYOR: It would seem to me that it is you who are doing all the daring, Thomas.

PETRA: This is a shocking way to treat a man like Father!

DR. STOCKMANN: Be quiet, Petra.

MAYOR: So we've got opinions of our own already? Well, I'm not surprised. *(to MRS. STOCKMANN)* Katherine, you appear to be the most sensible person in this house. Use what influence you may have with your husband and try to make him see what all this means, both for his family . . .

DR. STOCKMANN: My family is my affair and nobody else's.

MAYOR: Both for his family, I say, and for the town he lives in.

DR. STOCKMANN: I am the one who has the true welfare of the town at heart. I want to expose a disgraceful state of affairs that must come out sooner or later.

MAYOR: That's why you're intending to cut off the town's main source of revenue, I suppose.

DR. STOCKMANN: Don't you understand? The source is poisoned, man. Are you mad? We're supposed to be a health resort and we're selling dirt and disease! The whole of our flourishing social life is founded on a lie!

MAYOR: Any man who can make such insinuations about his own town is nothing but an enemy of the people.

DR. STOCKMANN: *(flaring up)* You dare to . . .

MRS. STOCKMANN: *(throwing herself between them)* Thomas!

PETRA: *(taking his arm)* Please, Father, don't.

MAYOR: You've been warned now. It's for you to consider what you owe to yourself and your family. Goodbye. *(exits)*.

DR. STOCKMANN: *(pacing)*. And to think I have to put up with this kind of treatment in my own house, Katherine. What do you say to that, eh?

MRS. STOCKMANN: It is shameful and disgraceful Thomas, really.

PETRA: How I would have loved to give him a piece of my mind!

DR. STOCKMANN: It's all my own fault. I should have stood up to him years ago; shown my teeth and bitten. And now, calling me an enemy of the people! Me, good God! I'm not going to take that lying down.

MRS. STOCKMANN: But, Thomas dear, when all's said and done, your brother has got the power . . .

DR. STOCKMANN: But I'm in the right.

MRS. STOCKMANN: Yes yes, the right; but what's the good of that if you haven't any might?

PETRA: Oh Mother, how can you talk like that?

DR. STOCKMANN: Are you trying to say that in a free society like ours, there's no point in being in the right? Don't be so ridiculous, Katherine.

MRS. STOCKMANN: For Heaven's sake, Thomas, you're not thinking of setting yourself up against your brother?

DR. STOCKMANN: What else do you expect me to do if not stand up for what's right?

PETRA: That's what I say!

DR. STOCKMANN: If they want a fight, they can have it, I'll fight to the bitter end.

MRS. STOCKMANN: And your family Thomas, what about them?

PETRA: Oh Mother, don't always think only of us.

MRS. STOCKMANN: *(to Petra)* Oh it's easy enough for you to talk. You can always look after yourself, but what about the boys, Thomas? *(They are now beside MRS. STOCKMANN)*

DR. STOCKMANN: If I give in to a coward like Peter and all his cronies, do you think I'd ever know a moment's peace the rest of my life?

MRS. STOCKMANN: I don't know about that, but what kind of life shall we have if you go on defying them? There you'll be again with no salary, no regular income and you know we've nothing else to live on. Didn't we have enough of that in the old days? Remember what they were like, Thomas. Just think what it'll mean.

DR. STOCKMANN: *(stuggling with himself)* And this is what those lackeys can do to a decent, honest man. Isn't it monstrous, Katherine?

MRS. STOCKMANN: It's disgraceful certainly, the way they're treating you, there's no arguing with that. But then, there's so much injustice one has to put up with in this world. There are the boys, Thomas. What's to become of them? *(EILIF and MORTON stand listening, holding their school books)*

DR. STOCKMANN: *(slowly standing erect)* Even if
    my whole world crashes about me, I shall never
    bow my head.

Cut to public hall: Mocking laughter, uproar.

ANGRY VOICES IN CROWD: Get that drunk out!
    Get rid of him!

DRUNK: Are you referring to me?

*Laughter, confusion and whistling. ASLAKSEN
rings his bell loudly. There is an uproar and the
drunk is ejected.*

MAYOR: Who was that person?

CPT. HORSTER: I've no idea, sir.

ASLAKSEN: The man was obviously intoxicated.
    Continue, Doctor, but do try to use a little restraint.

DR. STOCKMANN: Well, my fellow citizens, I won't
    say any more about our illustrious civic leaders. If
    anyone infers from what I've just said, that I've
    come here this evening to destroy these gentlemen,
    they would be quite mistaken — quite seriously
    mistaken — because it's my belief that these last
    survivors of a dying culture are perfectly able to
    destroy themselves. They have no need of me or
    anyone else to hasten their demise nor are they
    particularly the greatest danger to the community.
    They are not the ones most directly responsible for
    poisoning the sources of our spiritual life and
    contaminating the very air we breathe. No, it isn't
    they who are the most dangerous enemies of truth

and freedom in our society.

Cut to side stage: Editorial office of People's Tribune.

HOVSTAD: The real cause of all this evil is to be found in quite a different swamp.

DR. STOCKMANN: And what swamp would that be?

HOVSTAD: The swamp in which the whole of our communal life is rotting away.

DR. STOCKMANN: Really Mr. Hovstad, what kind of talk is this?

HOVSTAD: All the affairs of this town have gradually fallen into the hands of a small clique of bureaucrats and their cronies. It's the well-to-do; all the sons of those respectable families throughout the town. They're the ones who actually run this town.

DR. STOCKMANN: Perhaps so, but they are, on the whole, capable men with insight.

HOVSTAD: Did they demonstrate capability or insight when they laid the water pipes in their present position?

DR. STOCKMANN: No, of coure, that was very stupid of them, but all of that is going to be put right now.

HOVSTAD: And do you think they'll take kindly to

doing that?

DR. STOCKMANN: Whether they do or not, it has to be done.

HOVSTAD: If the press exerts its influence . . .

DR. STOCKMANN: That won't really be necessary, my dear fellow. I'm sure that my brother . . .

HOVSTAD: I'm sorry, Doctor, but I have to tell you that I have every intention of taking this matter up.

DR. STOCKMANN: In the paper?

HOVSTAD: When I took over the *People's Tribune,* I did so with the firm intention of breaking up this ring of bigots who wield all the power in this community.

DR. STOCKMANN: But you told me yourself that as a result, the whole paper was almost forced to close down.

HOVSTAD: Yes, we had to play things down at that time, it's true. There was a danger that if these men were ousted, the Baths might never be built. But now they're up, and all these high and mighty gentlemen can be dispensed with. What we must do is destroy the myth of infallibility that clings to these men. It is a superstition and must be eradicated like any other superstition.

ASLAKSEN: *(entering)* I'm right behind you, Doctor Stockmann.

HOVSTAD: *(explaining)* Mr. Aslaksen, the printer.

ASLAKSEN: I trust you'll forgive me for being so
bold, Doctor, but you might well find it useful to
have us tradespeople behind you. We form a pretty
solid majority in this town and when we want to
get things done, well, people have to take account
of us, and it's always a comfort, Doctor, to know
you have a solid majority behind you.

DR. STOCKMANN: I'm sure that's true, but I don't
really believe that any special measures will be
necessary in this case. It's all a perfectly
straightforward matter.

ASLAKSEN: I know these local authorities, Doctor
Stockmann. They don't take kindly to suggestions
from the outside. And that's why I thought it might
be quite appropriate for us to organize a little
demonstration.

HOVSTAD: Just what I feel.

DR. STOCKMANN: Demonstration?

ASLAKSEN: A moderate one of course, Doctor. I
always insist on moderation because, you know, in
a sense, moderation is a citizen's greatest virtue.
Now, as for this matter of the water works, it's of
great importance to ordinary tradespeople like
ourselves. The Baths look like becoming a little
gold mine for the town. We'll all be depending on
them for our livelihood, and that's particularly true
of us property owners. That's why we want to give
the project every support we can and as I'm the
Chairman of the Property Owners Association . . .

DR. STOCKMANN: Oh?

ASLAKSEN: Oh yes, I'm also on the board of the Civic Temperance Society. You do know I'm a longstanding temperance worker?

DR STOCKMANN.   Oh yes, yes.

ASLAKSEN: So naturally, I come into contact with a great number of people. I have a certain influence in the town, though I say it myself. I wield a little power here and there.

DR. STOCKMANN: So I believe, Mr. Aslaksen.

ASLAKSEN: Well, there it is. In any case, it would be a relatively easy matter for me to organize an address if the occasion should arise.

DR. STOCKMANN: An address?

ASLAKSEN: Yes, perhaps a kind of vote of confidence from the townspeople for your having promoted a matter of public importance; that kind of thing. Of course, it goes without saying, it would have to be couched in a suitable way so as not to give offense to the authorities.

HOVSTAD: Even if they were offended, it's high time that . . .

ASLAKSEN: No, no, no. On no account must we offend the authorities, Hovstad. There is no point in antagonizing people on whom we must rely for our day-to-day affairs. I've been all through that in my time and no good ever comes of it, believe me. However, the sober expression of liberal sentiments can cause no affront.

DR. STOCKMANN: *(shaking his hand)* My dear
Aslaksen, I can't tell you how touched I am to find
such great support among my fellow citizens. I'm
moved, quite moved and truly appreciative, but I
really can't see that all this fuss will be in any way
necessary. I would have thought the matter would
resolve itself quite easily, as a matter of course.

ASLAKSEN: The wheels of local government are
sometimes quite ponderous, Doctor, and may need
a little oiling from the outside.

HOVSTAD: We'll give them a blast in tomorrow's
paper that will make them shake in their shoes,
Aslaksen.

ASLAKSEN: But moderately, Mr. Hovstad. Proceed
with moderation at all times or you'll get nowhere.
(turns to DR. STOCKMANN) In any case, you can
be sure that the ordinary tradespeople of this town
stand behind you to a man. You have the solid
majority on your side, Doctor, *(takes DR.
STOCKMANN's hand and pumps it)*

Cut to public hall.

DR. STOCKMANN: Yes the solid, liberal, bloody
majority. They are potentially our most dangerous
enemy! Now you know!

*Complete uproar. Everyone shouts, stamps, whistles.
MRS. STOCKMANN rises anxiously. ASLAKSEN
rings his bell loudly and calls for silence. Everyone
in a tizzy. Finally silence is restored.*

ASLAKSEN: As chairman of this meeting, I call upon the speaker to retract his mischievous and ill-considered remarks.

DR. STOCKMANN: It is the majority in this very community that is attempting to deprive me of my freedom to speak the truth.

HOVSTAD: The majority always has right on its side.

BILLING: And truth as well, damn it.

DR. STOCKMANN: The majority is never in the right, never I say! That's just one of those deeply entrenched social fallacies which enlightened people have to fight against. After all, who constitutes the majority in any country, the wise men or the fools? I think you'd have to admit that all the world over, the fools are in an absolute and overwhelming majority. But in God's name, you can't honestly suggest that it's right and proper for the fools to govern the wise.

Cries, boos, general uproar.

Oh yes, you can shout me down but you can't prove me wrong. The majority has the power, the lung power as well unfortunately, but that doesn't make it right. It's I, and a few like me, who are right! It is the minority that's always in the right.

Renewed uproar.

HOVSTAD: So Stockmann's turned aristocrat overnight, eh Doctor?

DR. STOCKMANN: I've already said I've no intention
of wasting words on those feeble short-winded
flock of sheep that we are fast leaving behind us.
One can no longer make out the pulse of life in
their bloodstream. I'm talking about the few, those
few individuals among us who are still alive to the
young budding truths around us. Those few
pioneers of progress that stand, as it were, at the
outposts, so far ahead that the solid majority hasn't
yet been able to catch up with them. And there
they take their stand and fight for truths which are
too new in man's consciousness to have more than
a handful of supporters behind them.

HOVSTAD: So, now the Doctor's become a
revolutionary.

The crowd laughs, scoffingly.

DR. STOCKMANN: For once Mr. Hovstad, you're
actually right. I am in revolt against the lie that the
truth is always vested in the majority. For what
kind of truths are they that the majority favor?
Truths that are so old they creak at the joints! And
when a truth's as old as that, ladies and gentlemen,
it's well on the way to becoming a lie! *(laughter and
catcalls)* Yes, you may find it hard to believe, but
truths are by no means as old and hardy as
Methuselah. The life span of an average truth is
about seventeen or eighteen years, maybe twenty at
most. The more ancient they are, the more scraggly
they get and the less nourishing they are to the
community, and it's usually then that the majority
considers them fit for human consumption and
recommends them as good wholesome food. As a
doctor, I can assure you there's little nourishment
in that sort of diet. Majority truths are like last

year's salt pork or rancid old hams. The cause of all the moral scurvy that ravages society.

Cut to office of People's Tribune.

HOVSTAD: '. . . all the moral scurvy that ravages society!' Really forceful stuff, isn't it?

BILLING: Forceful? It's pulverizing. Every word falls like a sledge hammer.

HOVSTAD: We won't get them with only one broadside, you know.

BILLING: Then we'll keep on hammering away, blow after blow, till their whole empire collapses. Do you know, Hovstad, as I sat there reading those words, it was like hearing the first faint rumbles of the revolution.

HOVSTAD: *(turning around)* Sshh! For God's sake, don't let Aslaksen hear you talking like that!

BILLING: *(loudly)* Aslaksen is a *(suddenly hushed)* bloody coward. He's got the guts of a tape worm. You won't let him get his own way this time, will you? We're going to print this piece just as it stands, aren't we?

HOVSTAD: Yes, unless the Mayor butts in.

BILLING: The Mayor — that would be a bit of a bore.

HOVSTAD: But we can make the most of this situation either way. If the Mayor rejects Doctor Stockmann's proposals, he'll have the tradesmen

and townspeople down on him like a ton of b
the Property Owners Association, the Temperance
Society, the lot. And if he does accept them, he'll
fall foul of the shareholders of the Baths who've
been his strongest supporters up till now.

BILLING: Of course, because they'll have to fork out
quite a lot of money.

HOVSTAD: That's for sure, and that will sooner or
later break up the clique, and once that's done we'll
be able to show the public just how incompetent
the Mayor has been. And, of course, keep on
insisting that in the future, the Town Council,
indeed every responsible position, must be filled by
men of more liberal ideas.

BILLING: By God, that's true. It's coming! It's
coming! I can see it coming! We're standing on the
threshold of a revolution.

DR. STOCKMANN: *(entering rapidly)* Print away,
Mr. Hovstad!

HOVSTAD: It's come to that, then?

BILLING: Hoorah!

DR. STOCKMANN: Print away, I say. And not too
soon, either. If that's what they want, that's what
they're going to get. It's war now, Mr. Billing.

BILLING: To the death, I hope. Give them hell,
Doctor!

DR. STOCKMANN: This report's only the first shot.
I've already got four or five other articles on the

boil. Where's Aslaksen?

BILLING: *(rudely shouting)* Aslaksen!

HOVSTAD: On the same theme?

DR. STOCKMANN: One thing leads to another, you know. It's like pulling down an old building. Just like that.

BILLING: It's not finished till the whole bloody lot is down!

ASLAKSEN: *(entering)* Surely you're not thinking of pulling the Baths down, Doctor?

DR. STOCKMANN: No, nothing like that, Aslaksen. We were talking about something quite different. *(turns to HOVSTAD)* Well, what do you think about the piece, Mr. Hovstad?

HOVSTAD: It's a masterpiece. An absolute masterpiece.

DR. STOCKMANN: I don't think it's come off too badly myself.

HOVSTAD: It's so clear and concise, doesn't mince matters, and one doesn't need to be an expert to understand it. That's what I like. I'm sure you'll have every thinking person on your side once they've read it!

ASLAKSEN: And every prudent one too, I hope.

BILLING: And the imprudent ones as well. You'll have the whole town behind you.

ENEMY OF THE PEOPLE 149

ASLAKSEN: In that case, I should think we may venture to print it.

BILLING: I should damn well hope so!

HOVSTAD: It'll be in tomorrow's morning edition.

DR. STOCKMANN: Mr. Aslaksen, would you take personal charge of this manuscript?

ASLAKSEN: If you wish.

DR. STOCKMANN: Take the greatest possible care over it. No misprints. Every single word is important. I'll drop back later on, perhaps I could see a proof. I can't tell you how anxious I am to see it in print, actually fired off.

BILLING: Like a bombshell!

DR. STOCKMANN: You've no idea what I've been put through today. Threatened, harassed — deprived of my basic human rights! But now I'll give it to them, in black and white! I'll fight them every day if need be, in the columns of this paper. One broadside after the other . . .

ASLAKSEN: Yes, but remember . . .

BILLING: Hoorah, it's war, it's war!

DR. STOCKMANN: I'll beat them into the ground.

ASLAKSEN: But with moderation. It must be done with moderation.

BILLING: Don't spare the ammunition, I say!

DR. STOCKMANN: Because it's no longer merely a question of the water supply and drainage, you know. It's the whole of our public life that's got to be decontaminated, disinfected . . .

BILLING: That's the word for it. Exactly!

DR. STOCKMANN: All the old bunglers and bigots must go, all of them! Winnowed out of their cozy official nooks. It's the new young men we have to find to carry our banner, friends, to take command of all the old posts.

BILLING: Hear, hear!

DR. STOCKMANN: As long as we all band together, the change will happen as smoothly as a ship gliding from the stocks.

HOVSTAD: I think for the first time we have a real chance of getting municipal control into the right hands. At last!

ASLAKSEN: As long as we proceed with moderation, I don't foresee any great danger.

DR. STOCKMANN: Who the hell cares about danger? This has to be done in the name of truth and conscience.

HOVSTAD: You deserve every support, Doctor

ASLAKSEN: There's no doubt about it, the Doctor's a true friend of the town, a real asset to the community.

BILLING: He's a veritable champion of the people,

Aslaksen, and that's a fact.

DR. STOCKMANN: *(shaking hands with HOVSTAD and ASLAKSEN)* Thank you, thank you, my dear good friends. It does my heart good to hear this. My brother described me in very different terms this morning. Please take good care of the manuscript, Mr. Aslaksen, and for God's sake, don't cut out any of the exclamation marks. If anything, put in a few more. Good, good! Goodbye for now.

STOCKMANN shakes hands with them and leaves. The euphoric atmosphere gradually subsides in the ensuing pause. HOVSTAD crosses and sits on the edge of his desk, as does BILLING on his. ASLAKSEN warily examines the article in his hands.

HOVSTAD: He's going to be bloody useful to us.

ASLAKSEN: As long as he confines himself to the matter of the Baths, but if he goes far beyond that we'd be ill advised to follow him.

HOVSTAD: Hm. That all depends on . . .

BILLING: You're so damned timid sometimes Aslaksen.

ASLAKSEN: Timid? When it comes to local politics, I may well be a trifle cautious, Mr. Billing. I've learnt that much in the hard school of experience, let me tell you. But put me into a position of power against the government itself for instance, and then you'll see if I'm timid.

BILLING: No, no, I'm sure you're not. That's what I
    mean: you're so inconsistent.

ASLAKSEN: I have a very strong sense of what is
    practical, that's all. You can attack the government
    as much as you like without doing anybody any
    harm because, you see, it doesn't bother them.
    Once a politician is in, he's in. But the local
    authorities can be turned out, and then you might
    get an even worse lot in.

HOVSTAD: What about raising the level of the
    public through self-government?

ASLAKSEN: When a man has his own interests to
    protect, Mr. Hovstad, he's not all that concerned
    with democracy.

HOVSTAD: Then I hope to God I never have interests
    to protect!

BILLING: Hear, hear!

HOVSTAD: I'm no compromiser and I never will be.

ASLAKSEN: A politician should never commit
    himself, Mr. Hovstad. And as for you, Mr. Billing, I
    should take in your sails a bit if I were you, seeing
    that you've applied for the post of General Secretary
    to the Town Council.

    HOVSTAD turns to BILLING.

BILLING: I!

HOVSTAD: *You* Billing?

BILLING: Well, yes, but it was only to get at them, bring them down a peg or two . . .

ASLAKSEN: Well, it's none of my business, but if I'm accused of cowardice and inconsistency, I should like to point out that my record is there for all to see and if I've changed at all through the years it's only from having learnt the value of restraint and moderation. My sympathies have always been with the ordinary people but I don't disguise the fact that I have a certain respect for people in powerful positions, the local ones, in any case. (*exits*)

BILLING: It would be so nice to be rid of him, wouldn't it?

HOVSTAD: And who would foot the bill of our printing costs?

BILLING: It's a bloody bore not having any capital.

HOVSTAD: Yes, if we only had *that*.

BILLING: Couldn't we approach Doctor Stockmann?

HOVSTAD: He doesn't have a bean.

BILLING: No, but there's his father-in-law, old Morton Kiil, the one they call 'the badger'.

HOVSTAD: And what makes you think he's got any?

BILLING: There's plenty of money there! And some of it's bound to go to the Stockmann family. He's sure to provide for the children at least.

HOVSTAD: Is that what you're counting on?

BILLING: Counting on? I never count on anything.

HOVSTAD: And if I were you I wouldn't count on
that General Secreatry's post either because I can
assure you, you won't get it.

BILLING: Don't you think I realize that? Not getting
it is exactly what I want! I only applied out of sheer
cussedness. That sort of knock puts new fight into
you, gives you a fresh supply of venom. That's just
what one needs in a Godforsaken hole like this
where nothing ever happens.

HOVSTAD: Well, we'll see. We'll see. *(Returns to
work)*

BILLING: Well, they'll be hearing from me soon
enough. I better go and write that appeal for the
Property Owners Association. *(exits)*

*HOVSTAD straightens up at the desk. Looks
straight ahead.*

HOVSTAD: So that's the way the wind blows.

*Cut to public hall. Strong disapproving murmur
from THE CROWD.*

ASLAKSEN: It seems to me that our honorable
speaker has digressed somewhat from his original
point.

MAYOR: I must agree, Mr. Chairman.

DR. STOCKMANN: I'm sticking exactly to the

point! Because my point is precisely this. That it's the masses, the mob, the solid majority that's poisoning the sources of our public morality and infecting the very ground we walk on.

HOVSTAD: And all because the vast majority of discriminating people are sensible enough to accept well tried and indisputable truths?

DR. STOCKMANN: Rubbish, Mr. Hovstad. Don't talk to me about indisputable truths. The truths of the masses are the same ones that were considered to be advanced thinking in our grandfathers' day. We've outstripped them entirely today. I believe there's only one indisputable truth and that is that no society can live a healthy life on truths that are old and marrowless.

HOVSTAD: Instead of all this generalizing why don't you give us a few examples of these old and marrowless truths on which we're living?

Cut to editorial office. PETRA, book in hand. HOVSTAD walks into the scene.

PETRA: '. . . that there is a kindly providence which protects all the so-called good people of this world and turns everything to their advantage, and that all the so-called bad people are inevitably punished. You can't possibly print this in the *People's Tribune!*

HOVSTAD: Why not? That's just what people want to read.

PETRA: You don't believe a word of that yourself.

You know perfectly well that things don't happen like that in real life.

HOVSTAD: An editor, my dear Petra, can't always do as he pleases. From time to time he must indulge people's weaknesses especially in the more popular sections of his paper. After all, the important thing is politics — the editorial columns. If I want people to follow me in my more progressive views, then I mustn't scare them away. If, at the bottom of the page, they find a nice serial with a neat moral at the end, they'll be all the more inclined to cast a friendly eye on what's printed above.

PETRA: You're not really as devious as all that?

HOVSTAD: I thank you for having such a high opinion of me. But, in any case, this was Billing's idea, not mine.

PETRA: Billing? But Billing holds such progressive views . . . ?

HOVSTAD: Billing is a man of many parts you know. I've just heard for instance, that he's applied for the post of General Secretary to the Council.

PETRA: *(beat)* I can't believe that, Mr. Hovstad. How could he reconcile that with his political views?

HOVSTAD: You better ask him that.

PETRA: I'd never have thought that of Billing.

HOVSTAD: *(close to PETRA: she suddenly turns to him)* Wouldn't you? Is it so surprising? We journalists aren't really such an elevated lot, you know.

PETRA: Do you really mean that?

HOVSTAD: Yes, I do, on the whole.

PETRA: Well perhaps in one's ordinary, day-to-day
affairs, I can quite see that, but now that you've
taken on such a really great cause, it ought to make
you feel more significant than most people. It's
such a splendid profession to be in. Blazing away
for truth and brave new ideas! Taking up cudgels
for a man who's been wronged.

HOVSTAD: Especially when the wronged man is . . .
hmm . . . how shall I say . . . ?

PETRA: Such a man of honor and integrity.

HOVSTAD: No, I was going to say, especially when
he's your father.

PETRA: What?

HOVSTAD: Yes, Petra. Miss Petra.

PETRA: So that's what's behind it all for you? That's
what you're thinking of? Not the issue itself? Not
the truth? Not my father's loyalty to the
people . . . ?

HOVSTAD: Well, that as well, of course.

PETRA: You've let the cat out of the bag there, Mr.
Hovstad. I'll never be able to trust you again!

HOVSTAD: Can you be so offended with me when

it's mainly for your sake . . .

PETRA: I'm angry because you haven't been honest
with Father. You talk to him as if truth and the
good of the people were all you cared about.
You've been deceitful to both of us. You're not the
man you pretend to be, Mr. Hovstad. I shall never
forgive you for that. Never!

HOVSTAD: You shouldn't speak so harshly to me,
Miss Petra, particularly now.

PETRA: And why not now?

HOVSTAD: Because just now your father needs all
the help I can give him.

PETRA: So that's the sort of man you are!

HOVSTAD: I — I — I'm sorry. I didn't mean that.
Please believe me . . .

PETRA: I know what to believe. (*hurls down book at
his feet*) There's your book, Mr. Hovstad.

DR. STOCKMANN: Truths old! . . .

PETRA: You can give it to someone else.

DR. STOCKMANN: . . . and marrowless.

Cut back to public meeting.

*Murmurs and grumbles from THE CROWD under
DOCTOR STOCKMANN's speech.*

DR. STOCKMANN: I could reel off dozens of them

for you: all kinds of accumulated slime from the past. But I'll confine myself to just one; one acknowledged truth which is actually one of the most outrageous lies ever propounded, but on which Mr. Hovstad and the *People's Tribune* and it's readers are constantly nourished.

HOVSTAD: Really? — and what's that?

DR. STOCKMANN: It's a doctrine inherited from your ancestors which is still passed on mindlessly from one generation to the other. The doctrine that the common man, the mass man, the man in the street, is the salt of the earth and that he has as much right to approve and condemn, to counsel and to govern as the truly qualified, intellectually superior, elite.

BILLING: I'll be damned if I've ever heard anything . . .

HOVSTAD: Remember those words, ladies and gentlemen. Note them down.

SEVERAL VOICES FROM THE CROWD: *(scattered and angry)* So, we're not the people. It's only the posh people that can have a say . . .

WORKER: I'm not going to listen to that rot. Chuck him out!

ANOTHER: Into the street with him!

2ND CITIZEN: *(calling out)* Give him the horn, Evernson!

There is an enormous din full of horns, whistles,

boos and catcalls. During all of this, STOCKMANN leans his head onto his hand and waits for the uproar to subside.

DR. STOCKMANN: *(after noise has subsided)* I'm not asking you to agree with me all at once. But I must admit, I did expect that Mr. Hovstad would be on my side once he'd given the matter a little thought. After all, he does claim to be a free thinker!

SEVERAL VOICES FROM THE CROWD:
   (murmuring) Free thinker, did he say? Is Hovstad a free thinker?

HOVSTAD: *(shouting)* I challenge you to prove that statement! When have I ever said that in print?

DR. STOCKMANN: No, by God you're quite right there. You never did have the courage to say it straight out. Well, I certainly don't mean to embarrass you, Mr. Hovstad. Let *me* be the free thinker then and I'll try to prove to you all, scientifically, that the *People's Tribune* is only making fools of you when it tells you that the masses are the backbone of the nation. It's just another journalistic lie! The masses are nothing more than the raw material out of which, some day, true individuals may be fashioned!

Hubbub, jeers and laughter.

VOICE FROM THE CROWD: Three cheers for Hovstad!
Hurrah! Hurrah! Hurrah!

DR. STOCKMANN: Well, isn't that the way nature

works with all living creatures? Isn't there, for instance, a world of difference between a pedigree and an ordinary animal? Take the dog, man's best friend. Just picture an ordinary mongrel, one of those filthy, ragged curs that lope along the streets defiling the walls and lampposts. Compare him with a pedigree hound, brought up in a fine house, on good food, used to the sound of soft voices and music. Don't you think the brain of that animal is very differently developed from that of the mongrel? Of course it is! You've seen them yourselves, perfectly trained, performing all kinds of amazing tricks. A mongrel could never learn to do that sort of thing even if you stood it on its head.

CITIZEN: Are you trying to make out we're all dogs now?

ANOTHER VOICE FROM THE CROWD: We are not animals, Doctor.

DR. STOCKMANN: But that's just what we are, my friend, whether we like it or not! The very highest type of animal no doubt, but even among us, there are plenty of mongrels to be found. And that's what's so curious — that Mr. Hovstad is quite prepared to agree with me so long as we are talking about four-legged animals. But as soon as one extends the metaphor to two-legged creatures, Mr. Hovstad parts company with me. He hasn't the courage to carry his convictions to their logical conclusion. So he turns the whole argument upside down and tells you in the columns of the *People's Tribune* that the farmyard hen and the street mongrel are actually the finest specimens in our menagerie. But that's always the case as long as a man remains stuck in the mud of his old, inherited ideas and doesn't break through to a superior mental plane.

HOVSTAD: I make no claims to any superiority. I come from honest, hard working, country folk and I'm proud that my roots are with those very common people that you've just been insulting.

VOICES FROM THE CROWD: Hurrah! Good old Hovstad! Bravo! Hear, hear! Tell him where to get off!

DR. STOCKMANN: The kind of mob I'm referring to isn't always to be found in the bottom of the barrel. They swarm around us at every level, even the highest. Just take my brother for example, our own smug, sleek Mayor. He's as common as anything you can find crawling around on two feet.

Mocking laughter from THE CROWD.

MAYOR: I protest against these personal allusions.

DR. STOCKMANN: And that's not because he, like myself, is a descendant from an old, Pomeranian cutthroat of a pirate, for that's what we are.

MAYOR: Ridiculous gossip! Complete fabrication.

DR. STOCKMANN: It's because he takes all of his ideas from those immediately above him — and people who do that, intellectually speaking, belong to the masses no matter what their social position. And that's why my illustrious brother Peter is so essentially vulgar and has never managed to have an original thought in his head.

MAYOR: Mr. Chairman, is this kind of thing to be permitted?

THE CROWD laughs mockingly at MAYOR as he walks into next scene.

Cut to editorial office. MAYOR walks in confronting ASLAKSEN and HOVSTAD, places hat and stick on desk.

MAYOR: Are you intending to print this?

HOVSTAD: I can hardly refuse a signed article by so distinguished a . . .

ASLAKSEN: It's nothing to do with me, Your Worship. I only print what I'm given.

MAYOR: I see.

ASLAKSEN: And so, if you'll excuse me.

MAYOR: You've always been a very sensible person, Aslaksen.

ASLAKSEN: I'm glad Your Worship thinks so.

MAYOR: And a man of considerable influence, I may say, as well.

ASLAKSEN: Among a small group of working people perhaps.

MAYOR: The working people, the rate payers, form the majority here as elsewhere.

ASLAKSEN: I suppose that's true, Your Worship.

MAYOR: And I've no doubt you represent their views quite accurately on most matters, wouldn't you say?

ASLAKSEN: Yes, I think I may say I do.

MAYOR: It shows a remarkable public spirit for people of moderate means to contemplate such a heavy sacrifice.

HOVSTAD: I don't quite . . . sacrifice?

MAYOR: But then of course you're in much closer touch with public opinion than I am.

ASLAKSEN: Yes, but Your Worship . . .

MAYOR: And it's certainly no small sacrifice that the town will have to make.

HOVSTAD: The town?

ASLAKSEN: I don't quite understand, surely the Baths . . .

MAYOR: At a fairly conservative estimate, the alterations proposed by the Doctor will come to about one hundred thousand crowns. Naturally, we shall be obliged to raise a municipal loan.

HOVSTAD: You surely don't mean that the townspeople . . .

ASLAKSEN: You don't mean to say it's to come out of the rates? Out of the pockets of the small businessmen?

MAYOR: Where else is the money to come from?

ASLAKSEN: Surely that's a matter for the owners of
    the Baths.

MAYOR: The Baths Committee, I'm afraid, cannot
    see their way towards any additional expenditure.

ASLAKSEN: Is that quite definite, Your Worship?

MAYOR: I've examined the matter thoroughly. If the
    town wants all these extensive alterations carried
    out, it's the townspeople who will have to pay for
    it.

ASLAKSEN: But bloody hell, forgive me, Your
    Worship — but that puts a completely different
    complexion on the whole situation, Hovstad.

HOVSTAD: It certainly does.

MAYOR: But even worse than that, we shall be
    compelled to close the Baths for at least two to
    three years.

HOVSTAD: Close them? You mean close them down
    altogether?!

ASLAKSEN: For two years?

MAYOR: Two or three. That's how long we estimate
    the work would take.

ASLAKSEN: But bloody hell — I mean, good heavens,
    how are we property owners to live in the
    meantime?

MAYOR: That's a rather difficult question to answer, Mr. Aslaksen. But what can you expect? Do you suppose a single visitor will come here if we start putting about the rumor that our water is polluted, that the place is a hotbed of infection, that the whole town . . .

ASLAKSEN: Is that all it is then? A rumor?

MAYOR: With the best will in the world, I must say I've been unable to convince myself otherwise.

ASLAKSEN: But if that's the case, it's absolutely monstrous of Doctor Stockmann — I beg Your Worship's pardon but —

MAYOR: It's regrettable, Mr Aslaksen, I quite agree, but my brother has always been rather impetuous.

ASLAKSEN: *(truns on HOVSTAD)*. And you intend to support him in this wild scheme, Hovstad!

HOVSTAD: But who could have possibly known that . . .

MAYOR: I've drawn up a brief résumé of the situation as it appears to an impartial observer and in it I've suggested how the possible defects could perfectly well be put right without any great loss of revenue and with the means available to the Baths and the town.

HOVSTAD: Do you have it with you, Your Worship?

MAYOR: *(taking pages out of his pocket)*. Yes, I brought it along just in case you might . . .

ASLAKSEN: *(seeing DOCTOR STOCKMANN)*.
     Good God, there he is!

*MAYOR turns towards the lectern sees DOCTOR
STOCKMANN and hurriedly exits.*

*Cut to public hall: DOCTOR STOCKMANN
speaking.*

DR. STOCKMANN: And that's why I say, it's quite
     indefensible for the *Tribune* to preach day after
     day the false doctrine that it is the masses, the mob,
     the solid majority, that have a monopoly on
     liberalism and morality, and that vice and
     corruption and every other kind of spiritual filth is
     a kind of pus that seeps out of our culture just like
     all that pollution seeping down into the Baths from
     the tanneries up in Molledal.

*Murmurs and agitation from the crowd as
STOCKMANN moves upstage into the editorial
office.*

DR. STOCKMANN: *(fiery)* And there's another thing
     I want to tell you.

ASLAKSEN: *(conversationally)*. Couldn't it wait for
     another time?

DR. STOCKMANN: *(conversationally)*. It'll only take
     a minute. It's just this: when people open their
     papers tomorrow and read my article and discover
     I've been quietly working away for the good of the
     town all winter — I know and you know that it was
     no more than my duty as a citizen — but all the
     townspeople who think so much of me. . .

ASLAKSEN: Yes, they have thought much of you until now, Doctor.

DR. STOCKMANN: Well that's just what I mean — when they realize all this — especially the working people — it might be like a clarion call to take matters into their own hands.

HOVSTAD: Look, Doctor, I think I really ought to tell you that. . .

DR. STOCKMANN: Ah ha! Something's already afoot. I thought as much but I don't want it! If they're thinking of organizing something. . .

HOVSTAD: Like what?

DR. STOCKMANN: Oh anything — a torch-light procession, a banquet, a dinner — anything like that, you must give me your word to put a stop to it. And you too, Mr Aslaksen.

HOVSTAD: I'm sorry, Doctor, but before you go any further we'd better tell you.

Enter MRS STOCKMANN.

MRS. STOCKMANN: *(sees DOCTOR STOCKMANN).* Ah, just as I thought!

DR. STOCKMANN: What the devil are you doing here, Katherine?

MRS. STOCKMANN: You know very well, Thomas, *(turns to HOVSTAD).* Now you mustn't be angry that I've come to fetch my husband. I am the mother of three children, after all.

DR. STOCKMANN: Really Katherine, we know all that.

MRS. STOCKMANN: Well, you're not acting as if you do. You seem to have completely forgotten the fact that you've a wife and family. Dragging us into all this bother.

DR. STOCKMANN: Are you off your head, Katherine? Is a man to refuse to speak the truth because he has a wife and children?

MRS. STOCKMANN: Oh Thomas, if only you could learn some restraint.

ASLAKSEN: That's what I say, Mrs Stockmann. Restraint in all things.

MRS. STOCKMANN: And as for you, Hovstad — it's really a bad show luring my husband away from home and making a fool of him like this!

HOVSTAD: I'm not making a fool of anyone. . .

DR. STOCKMANN: Do you think I would allow myself to be made a fool of?

MRS. STOCKMANN: Oh, I know you're the cleverest man in town but sometimes you're also the biggest fool, Thomas. *(to HOVSTAD)*. Don't you realize he'll lose his job at the Baths if you print that thing he's written?

DR. STOCKMANN: Rubbish, Katherine! Now run along home and take care of the house and let me attend to society. How you can get yourself into such a state when you see me so full of confidence,

I don't know.*(rubs his hands and paces about)*. Truth and the people will win the day, you can be sure of that! I can just see all the townspeople full of solidarity, marching together like . . .*(stops by desk)*. What the devil's that? *(ASLAKSEN looks to desk as does HOVSTAD. DOCTOR STOCKMANN picking up MAYOR's hat:)* Well, if it isn't the sparkling symbol of authority! *(fingering the MAYOR's tophat)*.

MRS. STOCKMANN: The Mayor's hat!

DR. STOCKMANN: And his magic wand as well . . . *(picking up the MAYOR's stick)*. How in the name of. . .

HOVSTAD: Well —

DR. STOCKMANN: Ah ha! I see! He's been here talking you round! *(laughs)*. Well he's certainly come to the right place! And when he caught sight of me through the window, I suppose . . . *(bursts out laughing)* . . . he just bolted, didn't he Aslaksen?

ASLAKSEN: *(quickly)*. Yes, that's right, Doctor. He just bolted.

DR. STOCKMANN: Just took off leaving his . . . *(the penny dropping)*. Just a minute! Peter would never leave anything behind. That's not his style. *(looking about)*. Where is he? What have you done with him? *(checks drawers)*. In here? In there? We'll soon ferret him out, Katherine.

MRS. STOCKMANN: Thomas, please don't — I beg of you —

ASLAKSEN: I shouldn't if I were you, Doctor.

STOCKMANN puts on the MAYOR's hat and takes hold of his stick. Then turns to the upstage door, approaches it stealthily and suddenly whips it open revealing the MAYOR in the doorway. The MAYOR moves in with BILLING behind him.

MAYOR: And what is the meaning of all this?

DR. STOCKMANN: A little respect, if you please. I'm now in charge of the town. *(He struts up and down with the MAYOR's hat and stick).*

MRS. STOCKMANN: *(almost in tears).* Please, Thomas!

DR. STOCKMANN: You may be Chief of Police but I'm chief of the council, chief of the communities, chief of the whole town, the newly elected Mayor in fact!

MAYOR: Take off that hat!

DR. STOCKMANN: Pooh, do you think that the newly-born lion of the people will let itself be frightened by a little hat? We're going to have ourselves a revolution tomorrow. You're just in time for the party. You thought you could boot me out. Well now it's I who'll be booting you out — from all your offices and privileged positions! You think I can't! I can! I've got the whole power of society behind me! Hovstad and Billing thundering away in the *People's Tribune* and Mr Aslaksen will be leading the band with the whole of the Property Owners Association behind him . . .

ASLAKSEN: No, Doctor, I won't.

DR. STOCKMANN: Of course you will!

Pause. STOCKMANN looks at ASLAKSEN.

MAYOR: Perhaps Mr Hovstad will join your demonstration?

HOVSTAD: No, Your Worship.

ASLAKSEN: Mr. Hovstad's not such a fool as to ruin himself and his paper for a figment of someone's imagination.

DR. STOCKMANN: *(on table).* What's all this about?

HOVSTAD: You've presented your case in a false light and therefore I'm afraid I cannot possibly support it.

BILLING: And after what the Mayor has just told us I . . .

DR. STOCKMANN: False light! I take full responsibility. Just print the article and leave the rest to me! There isn't a word there that isn't true and I can prove it.

HOVSTAD: I'm sorry, Doctor, I cannot, will not, dare not, print it.

DR. STOCKMANN: Dare not? What kind of rubbish is this? You're the editor — the editor controls the paper, doesn't he?

ASLAKSEN: No, Doctor, the subscribers do.

MAYOR: Fortunately.

ASLAKSEN: It's public opinion, Doctor. The well-informed, general public, the landlords, the tradespeople — they're the people who are in control.

DR. STOCKMANN: And all those are ranged against me?

ASLAKSEN: It would mean nothing but ruin for the town if your article were to appear.

DR. STOCKMANN: I see. *(Pause; everyone slowly turns to STOCKMANN who is standing on the desk).*

MAYOR: My hat and my stick, if you don't mind.

STOCKMANN, slowly climbs down from the desk with the help of MRS. STOCKMANN, removes the top hat and hands it to the MAYOR, Then, without warning, tosses him the stick which he catches promptly).

MAYOR: Your term of office was rather short-lived.

DR. STOCKMANN: It's not over yet. *(to HOVSTAD).* You refuse, then, to print my article in the *People's Tribune?*

HOVSTAD: If for no other reason than in consideration for your family.

MRS. STOCKMANN: Never mind his family, Mr
      Hovstad.

MAYOR: *(taking papers from his pocket)*. The public
      will have all the necessary information when this
      appears. It's an official statement, Mr. Hovstad.

HOVSTAD: *(taking the papers)*. Right. I'll see that it's
      set up right away.

DR. STOCKMANN: I want this printed as a pamphlet
      at my own expense. I'll publish it myself! I want
      four hundred copies — five — no, make it six
      hundred copies.

ASLAKSEN: I wouldn't print it at any price, Doctor.
      I daren't. The weight of public opinion wouldn't
      let me. *(Beat. STOCKMANN takes it all in)*. There
      isn't a printer in town who would accept it,
      Doctor.

DR. STOCKMANN: *(taking it back)*.I'll see that it
      reaches the public all the same. I shall organize a
      mass meeting and read it myself. The citizens of
      this town shall hear the truth.

MAYOR: No one in the town will let you have a hall
      for such a purpose.

ASLAKSEN: No — you won't find anyone, I'm sure.

BILLING: No, by God, not in this town you won't.

MRS. STOCKMANN: This is disgraceful. Why are
      they all against you?

DR. STOCKMANN: I'll tell you why! It's because all

men in this town are old women! Just like you. All they can think of is their families and their safety.

MRS. STOCKMANN: Well I'll show you one old woman who can be a man — for once. Because I'm on your side, Thomas!

DR. STOCKMANN: The truth will out! If they don't give me a hall, I'll hire a drummer to march through the town with me. I'll read it on every street corner. *(crossing to public hall).*

Cut to public hall: crowd reaction grows over STOCKMANN's bridging speech.

VOICES FROM THE CROWD: Make him stand down! Shut him up!

DR. STOCKMANN: I'll shout out the truth at every street corner. I'll write it in the newspapers of other towns! The whole country will know what is happening here!

HOVSTAD: It sounds like all you want to do is ruin the town, Doctor.

DR. STOCKMANN: Yes, I would rather ruin it than see it prosper because of a lie!

ASLAKSEN: Those are strong words, Doctor.

Shouts and whistling. THE CROWD begins to grow unruly.

HOVSTAD: A man who is willing to destroy a whole community is nothing but an enemy of the people.

DR. STOCKMANN: What does it matter if a
community that lives on deceit is destroyed? I say,
'raze it to the ground'. People who live by lies
should be exterminated like vermin, otherwise the
whole community will be contaminated, with the
result that the whole community will deserve to be
ruined and if it comes to that, I would say from the
bottom of my heart, 'Let the whole country be laid
to waste! Let the whole population be
exterminated!'

Long Pause.

VOICE FROM THE CROWD: That's the talk of an
enemy of the people.

THE CROWD: *(slowly rising to a pitch).* Yes! He's an
enemy of the people! He hates his own country!
He hates the people.

*The din becomes unbearable. ASLAKSEN bangs his
gavel but is drowned out by the din. Eventually he
restores order.*

ASLAKSEN: Both as a citizen and as a human being I
am shocked by what I have heard here tonight.
Doctor Stockmann has revealed his true self in a
way that I would never have dreamt possible. I
must say, I support the general view expressed by
this assembly and therefore, I move the following:
'That this meeting declares Doctor Thomas
Stockmann, the Public Health Officer, to be an
enemy of the people.'

*Wild applause, cheers, shouts and catcalls. DOCTOR
STOCKMANN's family alarmed, slowly rise from
their seats and huddle together.*

DR. STOCKMANN: *(trying to shout them down).*
You idiots, fools, I tell you that . . .

ASLAKSEN: *(ringing his bell).* You're out of order,
Doctor Stockmann. You no longer have the floor.
A formal vote on the motion will now be taken. Do
you have the papers, Mr Billing?

BILLING: Both the blue and the white.

ASLAKSEN: Good. Hand them out to the voters. *(to
the crowd).* Blue means no; white means yes. I shall
go and collect the votes myself.

*HOVSTAD and BILLING distribute the papers to
the citizens in the aisle. The following dialogue takes
place in the auditorium.*

1ST CITIZEN: *(to HOVSTAD).* What's come over
the Doctor? What do you make of all this?

HOVSTAD: You know how impetuous he's always
been.

2ND CITIZEN: *(to BILLING).* Listen, you've been a
guest in his house. Has he taken to the bottle?

BILLING: I don't know what's happened to him.
There's always liquor on the table whenever anyone
comes.

3RD CITIZEN: I think he goes off his head now and
then.

1ST CITIZEN: Is there insanity in the family, I
wonder?

BILLING: It wouldn't surprise me.

4TH CITIZEN: It sounds like pure spite to me. He
      obviously wants his own back for something or
      other.

BILLING: I know he was after a rise some time back
      but he didn't get it.

VOICE FROM THE CROWD: That's what it is!

DRUNK: I want a blue one — and a white one!

VOICES FROM THE CROWD: It's that bloody
      drunk again! Throw him out! Get rid of him!

      *MORTON KIIL approaches DOCTOR
      STOCKMANN.*

MORTON KIIL: Well, Stockmann, now you see what
      comes of all your loony ideas.

DR. STOCKMANN: I've done what I had to do.

MORTON KIIL: What was all that about the tanneries
      at Molledal?

DR. STOCKMANN: You heard me all right. That's
      where all the muck comes from.

MORTON KIIL: From my tannery as well?

DR. STOCKMANN: Yours, I'm afraid, is the worst
      of the lot.

MORTON KIIL: And are you going to put that in
      your paper as well?

DR. STOCKMANN: I've no intention of hiding anything.

MORTON KIIL: You may have to pay dearly for that, if you do. *(exits)*.

FAT MAN: *(in audience)* Captain Horster. *(CAPTAIN HORSTER moves to the front of the stage)*. So, you lend your halls to enemies of the people?

CPT. HORSTER: I reckon I can do what I like with my own property.

FAT MAN: Then you won't object if I do the same with mine.

CPT. HORSTER: And what's that supposed to mean?

FAT MAN: You'll find out tomorrow.

PETRA: Isn't that the man who owns your ship, Captain Horster?

CPT. HORSTER: Yes it is. Never mind.

ASLAKSEN: *(mounting the stairs, ringing his bell for attention)*. Ladies and gentlemen, I wish to announce the result. By a unanimous vote, with one exception . . .

VOICE FROM THE CROWD: That's the drunk!

Everyone laughs. ASLAKSEN continues.

ASLAKSEN: . . . this meeting declares the Public Health Officer, Doctor Thomas Stockmann, an enemy of the people! *(the whole hall erupts with cheering and applause).* Long live our grand old town! *(THE CROWD cheers).* Long live our worthy and industrious Mayor who has so loyally put aside all family feelings. *(THE CROWD cheers).* I declare this meeting adjourned.

BILLING: Three cheers for the chairman, good old Aslaksen!
HIP HIP . . .

CROWD: HURRAY!

DR. STOCKMANN and family huddle on one side of the stage while the public murmurs continue).

DR. STOCKMANN: My coat, Petra. Captain, do you think you can find room for a few more passengers to the United States?

CPT. HORSTER: For you and your family Doctor, I'm sure we can find room.

DR. STOCKMANN: Good. Come on Katherine. Bring the boys.

MRS. STOCKMANN: Thomas dear, let's go out the back way.

DR. STOCKMANN: No, no back ways for me, Katherine. *(turns to the audience).* You'll hear more from this 'enemy of the people' before he shakes the dust from his feet. I'm not as forgiving as certain people, I don't say: 'I forgive ye, for ye know not what ye do'.

ASLAKSEN: That is blasphemy, Doctor Stockmann.

BILLING: By God, there's no low to which he won't sink.

VOICES FROM THE CROWD: Now he's threatening us *(from different parts of house)*. Let's smash his windows, throw him in the fjord. Yes, yes, duck him in the fjord.

THE CROWD grows loud and hostile. Horn blowing, whistles, catcalls, shouts. A tomato is thrown from somewhere and lands at STOCKMANN's feet. The noise of THE CROWD increases and eventually they begin to chant: Enemy of the people! Enemy of the people! Enemy of the people! *DOCTOR STOCKMANN and family walk down the center aisle of the auditorium while the chant is bellowed out by the crowd and the house lights come up.*

Interval.

PART II

Lights up on fully detailed set of DR STOCKMAN's study. Bookshelves, cupboards containing medicine bottles along the walls. Door upstage leads to outdoors. Another door, stage-right, leads to other rooms. In the back, there is a giant study-window of which all the panes of glass are shattered except two. The room is in disorder. It is morning. Outside, the day is grey and cloudy.

After a moment or two, a stone smashes through one of the two remaining panes of the window, shattering the glass and coming to rest on the carpet. After a few seconds, DR STOCKMANN (in dressing gown and slippers) comes out, inspects the damage, picks up the stone and philosophically examines it.

DR. STOCKMANN: *(calling out).* I've got another one for the collection, Katherine.

MRS. STOCKMANN: *(off-stage).* You'll have plenty more before you're done, I expect.

DR. STOCKMANN: *(places stone alongside heap of stone already on the desk)* I shall keep all these as souvenirs. They'll serve as reminders to Eilif and Morton and they'll inherit them from me when they grow up. *(notices window)* Hasn't that, what the devil's her name, you know, the maid, got hold of the glazier yet?

MRS. STOCKMANN: *(entering).* Yes, but he wasn't sure he'd be able to make it today. Randine said he daren't come because of the neighbors. *(about to leave; stops, returns)* Oh, a letter's come for you.

DR. STOCKMANN: *(looks to her).* Well, let's have it. *(opens and reads it).*

MRS. STOCKMANN: Who's it from?

DR. STOCKMANN: The landlord. Notice to quit.

MRS. STOCKMANN: *(beat).* I can't believe it. He's such a nice man.

DR. STOCKMANN: He daren't do otherwise, he says. It's 'against his principles . . . cannot help himself . . . respect for public opinion . . . mustn't offend'. *(Looks to MRS. STOCKMANN for a moment then crumples it up and tosses it aside)* Anyway, it's of no more concern to us. In a few hours, we'll be on the ship and off to the New World.

MRS. STOCKMANN: Are you quite sure we're doing the right thing, Thomas?

DR. STOCKMANN: Do you think I'm going to stay here where I'm been branded an 'enemy of the people', had my windows smashed in, and look at this, Katherine, they've even torn my trousers.

MRS. STOCKMANN: Oh, dear, and your best pair too.

DR. STOCKMANN: A man should never wear his best trousers when he goes out to fight for truth and freedom.

MRS. STOCKMANN: Yes I know, Thomas, they've behaved very badly here, but is that good enough reason to leave the country?

DR. STOCKMANN: Do you think it'd be any better in any other town? The rabble is just as odious everywhere else. There's nothing to choose between. Don't think I've got any illusions about America. I'm sure that country is just as rampant with solid majorities, mob rule masquerading as democracy and all the rest of that political humbug. If only there was a desert island somewhere going cheap . . .

MRS. STOCKMANN: But what about the boys, Thomas?

DR. STOCKMANN: You really are extraordinary, Katherine. Would you really like our boys to grow up in a society like this? You saw for yourself last night that half the people are lunatics, and if the other half haven't already lost their wits, it's because they're beasts and have no wits to lose.

MRS. STOCKMANN: Yes, yes, I know it's all wrong
but . . .

*Sound of someone at door. Both DR. STOCKMANN
and MRS. STOCKMANN stop and look anxiously
towards the entrance. After a moment, PETRA,
carrying books, comes in.*

MRS. STOCKMANN: Petra, are you back so early?

PETRA: I've got the sack.

MRS. STOCKMANN: The sack?

DR. STOCKMANN: You too?

PETRA: Mrs Busk called me in and gave me notice,
so I thought it would be best to leave right away.

DR. STOCKMANN: Quite right, too.

MRS. STOCKMANN: Who would have thought Mrs
Busk would do a thing like that. She's always been
so nice and friendly.

PETRA: I could see she didn't like doing it, but she
said she daren't do otherwise.

DR. STOCKMANN: *(scoffs).* 'Daren't do otherwise.'
That's priceless.

PETRA: It wasn't only that. She showed me some
letters she'd got this morning.

DR. STOCKMANN: Anonymous, no doubt.

PETRA: Yes.

DR. STOCKMANN: Naturally. Daren't sign their names.

PETRA: Two of them said a certain person who's been a frequent visitor here, said that I hold some highly emancipated views on various subjects . . .

DR. STOCKMANN: You didn't deny it I hope.

PETRA: Not on your life! The fact is, Mrs Busk holds some pretty emancipated views herself when we're talking together after school. Anyway, since everyone seems to be whispering about it, she didn't dare take the risk.

MRS. STOCKMANN: Just imagine — a 'certain person who's been a frequent visitor'. You see Thomas, that's the kind of thanks you get for your hospitality.

DR. STOCKMANN: Come on, let's pack the bags as quickly as we can. The sooner we're out of here, the better.

MRS. STOCKMANN: Sshh. There's someone in the hall.

Moment of shared tension, then PETRA moves to door, opens it. CAPTAIN HORSTER is revealed.

MRS. STOCKMANN: Oh, it's you, Captain Horster. Do come in.

CPT. HORSTER: Good morning. Thought I'd look in to see how everything was.

DR. STOCKMANN: *(shaking hands warmly with him)*. Thanks, that's very good of you.

MRS. STOCKMANN: And thank you for so much for seeing us safely home last night.

PETRA: Did you get home alright?

CPT. HORSTER: Oh, I managed. Most people's bark is worse than their bite.

DR. STOCKMANN: Yes, isn't it astonishing what cowards they are when it comes right down to it. Look, these are the stones they've thrown in through the window. Just look at them! Have you ever seen such miserable specimens? There aren't two decent size stones in the whole lot. Just a lot of pebbles. And they stood out there howling and swearing they'd beat the life out of me. But action — action — you won't see much of that in this town.

CPT. HORSTER: You should be glad on this occasion, Doctor.

DR. STOCKMANN: I suppose so, but it's irritating all the same. I shudder to think what would happen if it ever came to a real national crisis. Public opinion would vote with its feet and the solid majority would scatter like a flock of sheep. That's what's really depressing. But dammit, it's got nothing to do with me anymore. They've called me an enemy of the people. Fine. That's what I'll be then.

MRS. STOCKMANN: You'll never be that, Thomas, and you know it.

DR. STOCKMANN: Don't be too sure, Katherine. An ugly word can sometimes be as fatal as a spot on the lung. And that damned name: I can't get it out of my head. It keeps nagging at me like acid in the tummy. Only there's no getting rid of it with bicarb. It's too deep for that.

PETRA: Just laugh at them, Father.

CPT. HORSTER: They'll think very differently one day, Doctor.

MRS. STOCKMANN: That's true; as sure as we're all standing here.

DR. STOCKMANN: Well, perhaps they can bloody well think what they like. When do we sail, Captain Horster?

CPT. HORSTER: Well, that's what I came to talk to you about.

DR. STOCKMANN: Nothing wrong with the ship?

CPT. HORSTER: No, she's sound enough — but it doesn't look like I'll be taking her out this time.

PETRA: Surely you haven't been sacked as well?

CPT. HORSTER: (*smiling*) Yes, I'm afraid I have.

PETRA: You too?

MRS STOCKMAN shares a look with DR STOCKMANN.

DR. STOCKMANN: And all because I spoke out. If

I'd dreamt that anything like that might . . .

CPT. HORSTER: Don't you fret about it, Doctor.
I'll find a post soon enough. There's lots of
companies about.

DR. STOCKMANN: And that shipowner of yours is
independently wealthy; a man of property. God,
it's disgusting!

CPT. HORSTER: Oh, he's not a bad sort, normally.
He said he'd have liked to keep me on, if only he'd
dared.

DR. STOCKMANN: But he didn't dare. Of course
not.

PETRA: If only you hadn't seen us home, perhaps
this would never have happened.

CPT. HORSTER: I don't regret anything.

PETRA: *(taking his hand)* Thank you.

CPT. HORSTER: Anyway, there's something else I
wanted to say. If you're really set on leaving, I've
got another idea which might work out.

DR. STOCKMANN: Good. I don't want to stay here
a moment longer than we have to.

MRS. STOCKMANN: Sshh. Isn't that someone
knocking?

*There is a pause. PETRA goes to door. It opens
revealing the MAYOR in the doorway.*

DR. STOCKMANN: Ah, come in; come in.

MRS. STOCKMANN: Now Thomas, promise me
    you won't . . .

MAYOR: I'm sorry, I didn't know you were engaged.
    I'll come back later.

DR. STOCKMANN: No, no, please come in.

MAYOR: I wanted to have a word with you alone.

MRS. STOCKMANN: We'll go into the sitting room
    for a bit.

CPT. HORSTER: I'll come back later.

DR. STOCKMANN: No, why do that? Go in there
    with Katherine. I'll be with you in a moment. I
    want to hear more about that idea of yours.

CPT. HORSTER: Right then, I'll wait.

    *CAPTAIN HORSTER, MRS STOCKMAN and
    PETRA enter the sitting room PETRA trailing a
    baleful look to THE MAYOR. THE MAYOR
    removes his top hat and then looks towards the
    broken windows and then at DOCTOR
    STOCKMAN.*

DR. STOCKMANN: It's a bit drafty here today,
I'm afraid. Perhaps you'd better keep your hat on. I
wouldn't want you to catch cold.

MAYOR: Thank you, I think I will *(does so)*. I think I
    caught a bit of a cold last night.

DR. STOCKMANN: Really? I found it quite warm myself — almost too close for comfort towards the end.

MAYOR: I'm sorry I was unable to prevent the excesses of last night's meeting.

DR. STOCKMANN: Is that why you've come this morning, to tell me that?

MAYOR: *(taking out a large envelope)* No. I've come to give you this document. It's from the Baths Committee.

DR. STOCKMANN: My dismissal, I assume?

MAYOR: Yes, dated from today. *(hands the letter to DOCTOR STOCKMANN who does not take it. Eventually he places it on the table).* We're sorry it had to come to this but quite frankly, we daren't do otherwise — on account of public opinion.

DR. STOCKMANN: I've heard that phrase before today.

MAYOR: You have to try to see this from our standpoint. It would be quite unrealistic for you to imagine you could have any sort of practice here after last night.

DR. STOCKMANN: Are you so sure of that?

MAYOR: The Property Owners Association has circulated a petition to all its members urging them not to consult you and it's highly unlikely that a single householder will refuse to sign it — they just don't dare.

DR. STOCKMANN: No, I suppose not. But so what?

MAYOR: My advice would be to leave town for a
          while.

DR. STOCKMANN: As a matter of fact, the same
          thing had already occurred to me.

MAYOR: Good. Then when you've had, say, six
          months or so, to mull things over — and if you
          could bring yourself to write a few lines of apology,
          admitting you were mistaken, expressing some
          regret —

DR. STOCKMANN: I might then get reappointed,
          perhaps?

MAYOR: It's not out of the question.

DR. STOCKMANN: But what about public opinion?

MAYOR: Public opinion is rather fickle, Thomas, and
          to be quite frank, it would be of considerable
          importance to us to get some sort of admission
          from you in writing.

DR. STOCKMANN: Yes, that'd make you smack
          your lips, wouldn't it? Haven't you understood
          what I feel about that kind of deception?

MAYOR: When you said those things, Thomas, your
          position was rather stronger. You had reason to
          suppose the whole town was behind you.

DR. STOCKMANN: And now they're on top of me,
          is that it? Rubbing my face in the dirt! *(flares up)*
          Never, I tell you, never!

MAYOR: A man with a family ought to think twice
       about his . . . convictions. He has no right to
       behave as you're doing. No right at all, Thomas.

DR. STOCKMANN: No right! There's only one
       thing in the world a man has no right to do — and
       do you know what that is?

MAYOR: No.

DR. STOCKMANN: No, I'm sure you don't! Well,
       I'll tell you. A free man has no right to befoul
       himself like a beast. He has no right to behave in
       such a way that he would be entitled to spit in his
       own face because of his behavior.

MAYOR: And that would sound very plausible if
       there weren't another explanation for your
       obstinacy.

DR. STOCKMANN: And what exactly do you mean
       by that?

MAYOR: You know perfectly well what I mean. But
       as your brother and a man of the world, I would
       advise you not to put too much trust into your
       expectations . . .

DR. STOCKMANN: Expectations? What the devil
       are you on about?

MAYOR: Do you seriously expect me to believe that
       you're unaware of the terms Morton Kiil has made
       in his will.

DR. STOCKMANN: I know that what little he has,
       has been put aside for some foundation for retired

craftsmen — but what's that got to do with me?

MAYOR: Well, to begin with, 'the little he has' isn't so very little. Old Morton Kiil is a man of considerable means.

DR. STOCKMANN: Well, I must say, that's news to me.

MAYOR: Really? Then I suppose it's also news to you that a considerable proportion of his money is to go to your children, and that you and your wife will benefit from the interest on that capital for the rest of your lives. Hasn't he told you that?

DR. STOCKMANN: (stunned) No, I swear he hasn't. On the contrary, he spends most of the time grumbling about how heavily he's taxed — but are you sure of this, Peter?

MAYOR: I have it from a completely reliable source.

DR. STOCKMANN: But good heavens, that means Katherine's future is completely provided for and the children as well! I must tell her. (calls) Katherine! Katherine!

MAYOR: (holding him back) Sshh! Don't say anything about it yet.

MRS. STOCKMANN: (off-stage) What is it?

DR. STOCKMANN: Nothing, nothing my dear. Never mind.

Door closed offstage.

STOCKMANN: *(pacing up and down)* Provided for, for life! What a relief.

MAYOR: It shouldn't be. Morton Kiil can change his mind — and his will — any time he likes.

DR. STOCKMANN: But he wouldn't do that, Peter. The Old Badger's delighted that I've dealt with you and your respectable friends.

MAYOR: *(after a searching look)* Ah, that throws a new light on quite a number of things.

DR. STOCKMANN: What are you getting at?

MAYOR: It's obvious. The whole thing has been a carefully contrived plot between you and him. All those violent accusations against the authorities in the name of truth was simply the price you paid that vindictive old man for making his will out in your favor.

DR. STOCKMANN: *(dumbfounded)* Peter — you are the lowest worm I've ever encountered in all my born days!

MAYOR: Everything's over between us now. And you can take your dismissal as final. Now we know where we stand and we've finally got a weapon we can use against you. *(He goes)*

DR. STOCKMANN: *(shouts)* Katherine! Scrub the floors behind him! Get that girl — what the devil's her name — with the runny nose. Get the buckets, scrub it all over! Bring the disinfectant!

MRS. STOCKMANN: *(off-stage)* Hush Thomas, stop

shouting like that. Please.

Pause. STOCKMANN looks towards where THE MAYOR has exited; picks up one of the rocks from the table as if he is about to throw it towards the door. Strenuously controls himself, then as if cooling himself down, places it against his forehead and eventually replaces it onto the desk. He then trudges heavily towards the armchair, slumps into it and stares straight ahead with a glazed, somewhat defeated look. Long weary pause.

PETRA: *(entering from doorway)* Grandfather's here and says he'd like to speak to you privately.

DOCTOR STOCKMANN does not stir.

PETRA: Father, Grandfather's here. He wants to have a word with you in private.

DR. STOCKMANN: *(suddenly reawakening)* What? Oh yes, yes, of course. Come in Father.

MORTON KIIL enters, looks towards the broken window and moves slowly to the desk.

DR. STOCKMANN: What is it? Take a chair.

MORTON KIIL: No, I don't need any chair. *(looks away)* Nice and cozy here today, Doctor.

DR. STOCKMANN: Yes, isn't it.

MORTON KIIL: Very nice. Lot's of fresh air. Your conscience feeling in good health this morning, I suppose?

DR. STOCKMANN: Yes, it does.

MORTON KIIL: I thought it might. *(thumps his inside pocket)* Do you know what I've got in here?

DR. STOCKMANN: A good conscience too, I hope.

MORTON KIIL: Something much better than that. *(takes out a thick pocket-book, opens it and from his position at the desk exhibits it to STOCKMANN, slowly waving it up and down. Gradually, to get a better look, STOCKMANN moves over to the desk towards the papers)*

DR. STOCKMANN: *(recognizing them)* Shares in the Baths?

MORTON KIIL: They weren't hard to come by today.

DR. STOCKMANN: You mean you've gone out and bought . . . ?

MORTON KIIL: As many as I could afford.

DR. STOCKMANN: But, my dear Mr. Kiil, you know the state of those Baths — how could you?

MORTON KIIL: If you behave yourself like a sensible person you'll have those Baths on their feet again. You said last night that all the filth comes down from the tanneries and mine's the worst of the lot. If that's true then my father and his father before him have been polluting this town for over a century — like three angels of death. You don't suppose that I'm going to carry the shame of something like that without doing something about it?

DR. STOCKMANN: I'm afraid you'll have to.

MORTON KIIL: No thank you. I'm not letting my good name and reputation seep down into the sewers. They call me The Old Badger; I know, I've heard them. A badger's a kind of a pig, I believe. Well, I'll show them they've got the wrong name for me. I intend to live and die a clean person. *(pause)* You're going to make me clean, Doctor.

DR. STOCKMANN: I — ?

MORTON KIIL: Yes you, my dear son-in-law! Do you know what I bought these shares with? No, I suppose you don't — Well, I'll tell you — with the money I was going to leave Katherine and the children after I've gone. I've managed to put a little bit aside, you know.

DR. STOCKMANN: *(after a moment)* You've gone and done that with Katherine's money?

MORTON KIIL: That's right. Every penny of it's invested in the Baths now. I want to see just how mad you are, Thomas. If you stick to that theory of yours about this muck and microbes and invisible animals, or whatever they are coming down from my works, it'll be just like cutting strips of flesh from your wife's body and Petra's and the children's. No decent father would do such a thing — unless he really was mad.

DR. STOCKMANN: *(manically)* But I am mad. I am mad.

MORTON KIIL: Not when it comes to your wife and
     your family. Even you can't be as mad as that.

DR. STOCKMANN: *(looking at him)* Why on earth
     didn't you come and talk to me before you bought
     all this rubbish?

MORTON KIIL: What's done is done.

DR. STOCKMANN: *(agonizing)* If only I weren't so
     certain about it. But I know I'm right; I'm convinced
     I'm right.

MORTON KIIL: The more you go on like that,
     Thomas, the less these shares are going to be
     worth.

DR. STOCKMANN: How could you do such a
     horrible thing? Risking Katherine's money and
     placing me into this impossible situation! *(KIIL is
     smiling)* When I look at you I feel I'm looking at
     the devil himself.

MORTON KIIL: Well, I think I'd better be off now.
     But I want to have your answer by no later than
     two o'clock. *(bangs his stick twice)* If it's 'no', then
     all these shares will go straight to charity — and
     straight away, this afternoon!

DR. STOCKMANN: And what will Katherine get?

MORTON KIIL: Not one brass farthing!

     *He moves to exit. As he opens door HOVSTAD and
     ASLAKSEN are on the doorstep.*

Well, look who we have here.

DR. STOCKMANN: What the devil — have you actually got the gall to show your face around here?

HOVSTAD: Well, we do actually.

ASLAKSEN: You see, there's something we'd like to talk to you about.

MORTON KIIL: Yes or no — by two o'clock.

MORTON KIIL exits. ASLAKSEN looks knowingly to HOVSTAD.

DR. STOCKMANN: Well, what do you want? Make it short.

HOVSTAD: I can quite understand you feeling somewhat put out with us over that meeting last night, Doctor . . .

DR. STOCKMANN: Put out? Is that how you would describe it? You're nothing but a couple of cowardly, old women — both of you. You ought to be ashamed to show your face.

HOVSTAD: You can say what you like, Doctor. The fact is, we had no alternative. We couldn't do otherwise.

DR. STOCKMANN: You *daren't* do otherwise, you mean, don't you?

HOVSTAD: If you like.

ASLAKSEN: But why didn't you give us a hint beforehand, Doctor Stockmann. The slightest hint to Hovstad or myself.

DR. STOCKMANN: Hint? About what?

ASLAKSEN: About what was behind it all.

DR. STOCKMANN: Behind it all? What on earth are you talking about? I don't understand.

ASLAKSEN: *(nodding knowingly)* Oh yes you do, Doctor Stockmann.

HOVSTAD: There's no need to keep it secret any longer.

DOCTOR STOCKMANN looks from one to the other.

ASLAKSEN: Isn't it true, Doctor Stockmann, that your father-in-law's going around town buying all the shares in the Baths he can lay his hands on?

DR. STOCKMANN: He has bought some shares today but . . .

ASLAKSEN: It would have been more discreet to have got someone else to do it. Someone not quite so close to you.

HOVSTAD: And you shouldn't have used your own name. Then nobody need have known the attack on the Baths came from you. You should have taken someone into your confidence, Doctor Stockmann.

DR. STOCKMANN: *(staring from one to the other. The penny finally drops)* Is it conceivable? Can such things really happen?

ASLAKSEN: *(smiling)* Obviously they can. But really Doctor, they should be done with a little more subtlety.

HOVSTAD: And it's always better to have as few people involved as possible. As soon as one forms a partnership, there's bound to be problems.

DR. STOCKMANN: *(keeping himself calm)* In a word, gentlemen, what exactly do you want?

ASLAKSEN: I think Mr. Hovstad would be the best person to . : .

HOVSTAD: No Aslaksen, it would be best if you do . . .

ASLAKSEN: Well, the fact is, now that we understand the way the land lies, we think it might be quite possible to put the *People's Tribune* at your disposal.

DR. STOCKMANN: But how can you dare to do that, Mr. Aslaksen? What about public opinion? Aren't you afraid it might cause a storm?

HOVSTAD: We shall have to ride out that storm.

ASLAKSEN: But you'll have to be quick off the mark, Doctor, as soon as your campaign has succeeded.

DR. STOCKMANN: As soon as my father-in-law and I have cornered all the shares you mean?

HOVSTAD: I assume your motivation is largely scientific in taking over the management of the Baths.

DR. STOCKMANN: Of course it's in the interests of science that I got the old badger to come in with me on this. What we'll probably do, is patch up the water pipes a bit, dig a few holes on the beach here and there and it won't cost the rate payers more than a few pennies. That'll do the trick, don't you think?

HOVSTAD: It sounds good to me so long as you have the *People's Tribune* behind you.

ASLAKSEN: In a free country like ours, you know Doctor, the press is a power to be reckoned with.

DR. STOCKMANN: Naturally, and so, of course, is public opinion. I'm sure Mr. Aslaksen, you will be able to square the Property Owners Association?

ASLAKSEN: Both the Property Owners Association and the Temperance Society, be assured of that.

DR. STOCKMANN: But gentlemen, I'm not quite sure how to broach this, but what kind of consideration do you . . .

HOVSTAD: Naturally we would prefer to give you our support gratis, but unfortunately, *the Tribune* is going through a rather sticky period — the circulation's not what it used to be. It would be tragic for that paper to close now when there's so much work that needs to be done in the social and political sphere.

DR. STOCKMANN: Of course. It would be very
        hard for liberals like ourselves. *(pause. nods,
        cogitates, suddenly explodes)* But I'm an enemy of
        the people! Don't you remember? An enemy of the
        people! *(rushes about the room)* Where's that stick
        of mine? Where the devil did I put that stick?

HOVSTAD: What do you mean?

ASLAKSEN: Surely you're not thinking of . . .

DR. STOCKMANN: *(manically)*And suppose I
        decide not to give you a single penny from all my
        shares? We wealthy people are quite tight with our
        money, you know?

HOVSTAD: You must realize that this business of
        the shares could be easily misconstrued.

DR. STOCKMANN: Misconstrued? Yes, that would
        be right up your street. Misconstruction. Unless I
        rescue the courageous *People's Tribune,* you'll put
        the worst possible construction onto it. Never give
        me a moment's peace. Vilify me, hound me down,
        throttle me as the hound throttles the hare.

HOVSTAD: It is the law of nature, Doctor, the law of
        self-preservation.

ASLAKSEN: One has to take one's food where one
        finds it, you must admit.

DR. STOCKMANN: Go and look for yours in the
        gutter! *(chases them around the room)* We'll soon
        see who is the strongest animal between the three
        of us. *(Grabs umbrella — begins to brandish it)*
        We'll see! We'll see!

HOVSTAD: You're surely not going to . . .

ASLAKSEN: Be careful with that umbrella, Doctor!

DR. STOCKMANN: Out, out you go Hovstad! — go on, jump for it!

HOVSTAD: *(trying to defend himself)* Have you gone mad?

DR. STOCKMANN: Out, out! — and you too, Aslaksen! Jump, I say! Up with your feet!

ASLAKDSEN: *(being chased)* Moderation Doctor, moderation! I'm not a strong man, you know. My heart is not . . . Help! Help! Help!

MRS. STOCKMANN, CAPTAIN HORSTER and PETRA enter from the living-room.

MRS. STOCKMANN: In heavens name, Thomas, what's going on here?

DR. STOCKMANN: *(brandishing umbrella)* Jump, I say! Go on, jump! Into the gutter!

HOVSTAD: Attempted assault! Unprovoked assault! I call you to witness, Captain Horster. *(runs out through the door)*

MRS. STOCKMANN: Thomas please, control yourself . . .

DR. STOCKMANN: Dammit, they got away!

ASLAKSEN, who has run into the wrong door, slowly emerges, is confronted with the furious

*DOCTOR STOCKMANN, screeches and exits
through the up-stage door with DOCTOR
STOCKMANN throwing the umbrella after him.*

MRS. STOCKMANN: What's happened? What have
    they done?

DR. STOCKMANN: I'll tell you later. I've got more
    important things to do right now. *(rushes to desk
    and begins scribbling furiously onto a visiting card)*
    Look at this Katherine what does it say?

MRS STOCKMANN: 'No, No, No,' — what does
    that mean?

DR. STOCKMANN: I'll tell you that later too. Petra,
    call that runny-nosed girl, whatever her name is,
    and tell her to go round to the Old Badger and
    drop this off as quickly as she can. Hurry now.
    (PETRA exits quickly with the card) Damned if I
    haven't had a visit today from every one of the devil's
    disciples. But now they're going to find out the pen
    is mightier than the umbrella! I'll dip it in vinegar
    and venom and throw the inkpot straight at their
    heads!

MRS. STOCKMANN: But Thomas, we're leaving.

PETRA re-enters.

DR. STOCKMANN: Well?

PETRA: She's taken it.

DR. STOCKMANN: Good. Going away, do you say?
    No by God. We're not going anywhere. We're
    staying right where we are.

PETRA: Staying?

MRS. STOCKMANN: In this town?

DR. STOCKMANN: *(intoxicated)* Yes, right here.
This is the appointed place. This is where the
battle is to be fought and this is where it's going to
be won! Soon as I get these trousers sewn-up, I'm
going into town to look for a house. We've got to
have some kind of roof over our head.

CPT. HORSTER: If that's all you want, you can have
my house.

DR. STOCKMANN: Can we? Really?

CPT. HORSTER: There's plenty of room and anyway,
I'm hardly ever there.

MRS. STOCKMANN: *(confused)* That's, well, that's
very good of you but . . .

PETRA: Oh, thank you.

DR. STOCKMANN: *(shaking his hand)* Thank you,
thank you. *(pauses, distracted for a moment)* Well,
that's one thing less to think about. Now I can get
to work! You've no idea how much there's to be
done, Katherine. Fortunately, having been
dismissed from the Baths, I've had plenty of time
to attend to everything. And can you imagine, they
want to take away my practice as well? Well,
they're welcome to it! I'll keep all my poor patients;
the ones that can't pay — damn it, they're the ones
who need me most anyway. But by God, they'll
have to listen to me! I'll preach to them morning,
noon and night.

MRS. STOCKMANN: *(perturbed)* Oh Thomas,
surely you've seen how little good preaching does.

DR. STOCKMANN: *(abruptly)* Don't be ridiculous,
Katherine! Do you think I will allow myself to be
beaten by public opinion, the solid majority and all
the rest of that rubbish? No thank you! *(muttering
incoherently to himself)* What I want to do is clear,
simple and straightforward. I want to drum it into
their idiotic heads that these so-called liberals are
the most insidious enemies of freedom — that
party platforms only smother the truth, however
vital it is and that expediency and self-interest turn
morality and justice upside down so that, in the
end, life becomes intolerable. *(turning suddenly to
THE CAPTAIN)* Damn it all, I ought to be able to
get that through their thick skulls, don't you think,
Captain Horster?

*CAPTAIN HORSTER looks doubtfully at
STOCKMANN.*

CPT. HORSTER: I suppose so. I'm not very up on
these kinds of things . . .

DR. STOCKMANN: *(muttering to himself)* It's the
leaders, the party leaders — they're the ones that
have to be rooted out! Party leaders are like hungry
wolves — they need to devour a certain number of
lambs every year in order to exist. Take Hovstad
and Aslaksen for example. How many innocent,
young idealists have they swallowed up? Or else
they mangle and maul them till they're fit for
nothing else but to be property owners or
subscribers to *The People's Tribune. (half sits on
desk; looks straight out to the audience)* Come here,
Katherine! Look at all that glorious sunshine.

Smell that marvellous fresh spring — isn't it wonderful?

Outside the day is grey and sunless. There is no spring air. MRS. STOCKMANN looks to CAPTAIN HORSTER, clearly frightened by DOCTOR STOCKMANN's odd manner.

MRS. STOCKMANN: If only we could live on fresh air and sunshine, Thomas.

DR. STOCKMANN: We may have to pinch and scrape a bit, but we'll manage somehow. I'm not worried at all about that. No, what really worries me is who is going to be firm and courageous enough to carry on the work after I'm gone.

PETRA: *(after a look to Mrs. Stockmann)* I wouldn't worry about that, Father. You've years and years ahead of you yet.

Eilif and Morton enter from the upstage door.

MRS. STOCKMANN: Have you got a holiday today then?

MORTON: No, but we had a fight with some of the other boys in the morning-break.

EILIF: That's not true! It was the others that started fighting us.

MORTON: Alright then, — and then Mr. Rorlund told us we'd better stay home for a few days.

DR. STOCKMANN: *(snapping his fingers)* That's it! I've got it! By God, I've got it! Neither of you will set foot in that school ever again.

THE BOYS   Never — ? Not go back to school?

MRS. STOCKMANN: *(agitated)* But Thomas . . .

DR. STOCKMANN: Never, I say! I'll teach you myself. That's to say, you won't learn a single God-given thing.

BOYS: *(clapping hands)* Hurrah! Hurrah!

DR. STOCKMANN: I'll make you free men instead. True aristocrats. I'll need your help, Petra.

PETRA: *(looks uneasily towards her mother before replying humoringly)* Yes Father, of course.

DR. STOCKMANN: And we'll start our school in the very hall where they branded me an enemy of the people. But we need more pupils. At least a dozen to begin with.

MRS. STOCKMANN pauses, looks at PETRA who returns her look of concern.

MRS. STOCKMANN: You won't find them in this town, Thomas.

DR. STOCKMANN: We'll see. *(to the boys)* Do you know any street urchins — real guttersnipes?

EILIF: Oh yes Father, I know lots!

DR. STOCKMANN: Good. I want you to get hold of them for me. I'm going to do some experiments with mongrels for once. Sometimes they've got some native intelligence.

EILIF: But what will happen when we become aristocrats?

DR. STOCKMANN: Then my boys, we'll chase all
    the wolves into the wilderness and they'll never be
    seen again.

EILIF and MORTON clap and cheer.

MRS. STOCKMANN: *(trying to calm his hysteria)*
    Let's hope the wolves won't drive you away first,
    Thomas.

DR. STOCKMANN: Are you mad, Katherine? Drive
    me away? Now — when I'm the strongest man in
    town.

MRS. STOCKMANN: *(genuinely worried by his
    manner)* The strongest? Now?

DR. STOCKMANN: Yes. In fact. I'd go so far as to
    say I'm one of the strongest men in the whole
    world.

BOYS: *(clapping)* Hoorah!

MRS. STOCKMANN: *(abruptly silencing them)* Sshh!

DR. STOCKMANN: *(lowering his voice)* Now, you
    mustn't tell anyone about it — not yet anyhow —
    but I've made a truly great discovery. *(gathers them
    all about him)* The fact is you see, that the strongest
    man in the world is he who stands most alone.

*MRS STOCKMANN looks with growing concern at
DOCTOR STOCKMANN, then turns to PETRA
who is obviously distressed. EILIF and MORTON
are confused. They look about. DOCTOR
STOCKMANN looks towards the window. Walks
to the table, takes up a rock and hurls it through the
glass, shattering it. THE BOYS applaud the*

suddenness and violence of the action. MRS STOCKMANN and PETRA look apprehensively at DOCTOR STOCKMANN, then at each other. STOCKMANN looks to them, hoping they will support his new-found confidence, but he finds only worried and agitated faces. He then turns to the desk and hurriedly gathers together all the stones, heaps them into his hands and walks towards the armchair, shielding them from the view of the others. Once in the armchair, he sits, staring straight out and takes on a strange, glazed expression. EILIF and MORTON look confusedly to their mother and start to move towards him. MRS. STOCKMANN stops them, throws a look to CAPTAIN HORSTER who interprets it and hastily ushers the children out of the room. MRS. STOCKMANN then puts her arm around PETRA's shoulder to get her to leave, but she shakes it off and continues watching her father hypnotically. MRS. STOCKMANN then quietly leaves the room, PETRA still focussed on DR. STOCKMANN who remains lost in thought, his eyes glazed. After a few seconds, the stones in his hands slowly begin to trickle through his fingers onto the floor — very, very slowly, one after the other. PETRA watches them fall, looks again at the impenetrable expression on her father's face, turns resolutely and hurries out of the room. The stones continue to trickle through DR. STOCKMANN's fingers as his gaze remains fixed and his eyes wide and staring. When the last of the rocks have fallen to the floor, the lights fade on the armchair and then, trailing, on the broken window — so that the last sight we see is the broken, jagged window panes in the background dissolving into black.

Fade out to black.

Curtain.

THE FATHER

A Free Adaptation from Strindberg

CAST

THE CAPTAIN, Adolph
LAURA, the Captain's Wife
NOJD
THE PASTOR
GRANDMOTHER
BERTHA, the Captain's Daughter
DR. OESTERMARK
NURSE, Margaret

DIRECTOR'S NOTE

A good part of this production is conceived from the
Captain's standpoint and what the audience sees on the
stage is what is filtered through that character's paranoid
and tortured sensibility. The play's tableaux and those
scenes designated to be played in red lighting belong to a
different style of playing from the rest. To make sense of
these shifts of style, actors and director must be aware that
something removed from naturalistic playing is intended.
Without observing these changes, the performance can
easily look quirky and confused.

C.M.

Lights up:

THE CAPTAIN, *trussed-up in a straitjacket, seated upstage, before a tall, gaunt door, looking fixedly ahead.*

Lights up:

LAURA, *centre left. She stands expectantly staring out front. From behind, she is slowly encircled by a soldier's arms. She struggles coquettishly for a moment but is subdued by the soldier's strength. We then see NOJD's face as it becomes visible behind LAURA's head. He brings his face around and kisses her cheek. She responds to this with a sly, seductive smile.*

Suddenly, the soldier's hands encircle her breasts and squeeze hard. She tries in vain to resist. Her skirts are rudely thrown up and she is penetrated from behind. Writhing in pain, she opens her mouth as if to scream. No sound is heard.

The lights fade out on her terrible expression.

Lights up:

THE PASTOR, *upstage. Back to audience. He stands for a moment, waiting.*

CAPTAIN: *(off-stage)* Send Nojd in here.

VOICE: *(off-stage)* Yes sir!

THE CAPTAIN *enters.*

PASTOR: What's it all about?

CAPTAIN: Oh, he's been at the servants again, the scoundrel.

PASTOR: Wasn't he the one who gave you all that trouble last year?

CAPTAIN: Ah, you remember do you? Look, can't you give him a talking-to. That might achieve something. I've cursed him, dressed him down even beaten him — all to no avail.

PASTOR: So now you want me to preach at him. You know the word of God never penetrates a soldier's armor.

CAPTAIN: I know it never penetrated mine. However, with him, anything is worth a try.

NOJD enters. Stands at attention before THE CAPTAIN.

Now what have you been up to, Nojd?

NOJD: I don't think I could go into that right now, sir. *(looks uneasily at THE PASTOR)*

PASTOR: Don't mind me.

CAPTAIN: Out with it.

NOJD: *(after another look)* Well, you see sir, it was like this. We was at this dance at Gabriel's and then Ludwig said to us . . .

CAPTAIN: We're not talking about Ludwig.

NOJD: Well then, Emma said maybe we should all go
          into the barn.

CAPTAIN: Are you saying it was Emma that seduced
          you?

NOJD: Well practically, sir. I mean, nothing ever
          happens unless the girl is willing.

CAPTAIN: Get to the point. Are you or are you not
          the child's father?

NOJD: I don't rightly know.

CAPTAIN: You what?

NOJD: One can never be sure.

CAPTAIN: Weren't you the only one?

NOJD: *That* time, but that don't mean to say I was
          the only one.

CAPTAIN: Are you saying it was Ludwig then?

NOJD: It isn't easy to say who it was for sure.

CAPTAIN: Did you or did you not tell the girl you
          want to marry her?

NOJD: *(look to PASTOR)* Well, you have to say that,
          sir.

GRANDMOTHER: *(to PASTOR, bemused)* He's
          absolutely incorrigible.

PASTOR: Now look here, Nojd. You're man enough

to admit that you're the father of the child.

NOJD: I admit I went with her, Your Reverence, but that don't necessarily mean that anything happened.

PASTOR: Don't be evasive. You don't want the girl to be left alone with a child, do you? We can't force you to marry her, of course, but you must accept the responsibility for the child. That's the least you can do.

NOJD: Then Ludwig must pay his share as well.

CAPTAIN: I can't work it out. It will have to go to court. There's nothing else for it. Dismissed.

NOJD doesn't move.

Get out!

PASTOR: Just a moment. *(approaching NOJD)* Don't you see that it's disgraceful to leave a girl high and dry like that. That such behavior is . . .

NOJD: If I knew for sure I was the child's father, Your Reverence, it'd be a different matter. But that's something you can never be sure of, and it's no fun sweating your guts out, if you don't mind my saying so, Your Reverence, for someone else's child. I'm sure you and the Captain would agree with that!

CAPTAIN: Get out!

NOJD: Sir! *(salutes and exits.)*

CAPTAIN: And stay away from the kitchen maid, do you hear! If you know what's good for you.

NOJD: Yes sir! *(exits)*

CAPTAIN: Well, I must say, you really laid into him.

PASTOR: I thought I was quite blunt.

CAPTAIN: You just sat there muttering.

PASTOR: Well what can one say? It's bad luck on the girl, yes, but it's just as bad on the boy. Suppose he isn't the father? The girl can suckle the girl at an orphanage for a few months and she's shot of it, but it's not so simple for him. She'll get a respectable position after it's all over, but if he gets chucked out of his regiment, his life is ruined.

CAPTAIN: It's all too complicated for me. I don't suppose for a moment the boy is innocent — although one can never be sure. If anyone's guilty, it's certainly the girl.

PASTOR: I don't condemn anyone. As you say, it's just too difficult to tell. But look, before we got dragged into all this paternity business, we were talking about Bertha's confirmation.

CAPTAIN: *(returning to his preoccupation)* It's not just the confirmation. It's the whole question of her upbringing. This house is teeming with women, everyone with a different theory about my daughter. My mother-in-law wants to turn her into a spiritualist; Laura wants her to be an artist; her governess is resolved she'll be a Methodist; old Margaret wants her to be a Baptist and the maids

are trying to drum her into the Salvation Army.
They're trying to piece her together like a patchwork
quilt. It's up to me to decide her future, surely, and
at every turn, I'm obstructed. I've got to get her
out of here.

PASTOR: There does seem to be a wilderness of
women in this house.

CAPTAIN: They're like a pack of tigers. If I didn't
keep them at bay with a redhot iron, they'd claw
me to the ground.

PASTOR laughs.

Oh yes, very funny — for you! It's not enough I
married your sister, you had to land me with your
stepmother as well.

PASTOR: You don't expect me to live under the
same roof as my stepmother?

CAPTAIN: But one's mother-in-law is all right? Yes,
so long as it's under someone else's roof.

PASTOR: Well, we all have our cross to bear.

CAPTAIN: Yes, but I've got yours as well. And then
there's old Margaret, still treating me as if I was in
diapers. Oh, she's a good old soul I suppose, but
the fact remains — she shouldn't still be here.

PASTOR: Keep the women in their place, Adolf.
Don't let them run you.

CAPTAIN: And how does one do that, pray tell?

PASTOR: I know Laura's my sister and perhaps I shouldn't be the one to say it, but the fact is she's always been a difficult child.

CAPTAIN: Oh, she has her moods all right, but deep down she's not that bad.

PASTOR: I know her, Adolf.

CAPTAIN: She's been brought up as something of a romantic and so it's not all that easy for her to adapt to the realities of life, but she is my wife . . .

PASTOR: She's also your albatross, Adolf.

CAPTAIN: Yes, well, in any case, the whole thing has got badly out of hand. Laura refuses to cut Bertha loose and I refuse to let her stay in this madhouse.

PASTOR: I know how difficult it can be. Better than you. *(reflects)* When she was a child, Laura used to have a favorite game — playing dead. She'd just lie there — like a corpse — until she got whatever it was she wanted. And when she *did* get it, she'd give it right back saying it wasn't the *thing* she wanted. She just wanted to have her own way.

CAPTAIN: Was she already like that — even then? Hm. She gets so wrought up sometimes, it's quite frightening. I sometimes wonder if she isn't . . . well . . . disturbed.

PASTOR: What is it that's causing all the dispute? Surely there's ground for compromise.

CAPTAIN: I've no intention of turning the girl into a prodigy or a copy of myself or anything like that.

But I refuse to let her become a procurer and train herself just to make a good catch. If I did that and she didn't marry, she'd only become an embittered old spinster. On the other hand, I don't want her to have a vocation that requires years of study which will all be wasted if she *does* get married.

PASTOR: What do you want then?

CAPTAIN: I'd like her to be a teacher. If she doesn't marry, she'll be able to support herself. And if she does, she can use her education to bring up her own family. That sounds logical, doesn't it?

PASTOR: Quite. But what about her talent for painting. Surely one should encourage that.

CAPTAIN: I've shown her canvasses to established artists and it's nothing more nor less than amateur standard. Quite run-of-the-mill stuff. Then last summer, some jackass who pretended to be a great connoisseur comes along and calls her a genius. That's all Laura needed. The matter was settled once and for all.

PASTOR: Did he fancy the girl?

CAPTAIN: What do you think?

PASTOR: If that's the idea she's got in her head, God help you. And Laura's not short of allies in there.

CAPTAIN: Don't I know it! The whole house is like a battle-zone and between you and me, they're not exactly observing the rules of war.

PASTOR: *(to himself)* I've been through it all.

CAPTAIN: Have you?

PASTOR: Does that surprise you?

CAPTAIN: What's so maddening is that Bertha's
future is being influenced by the crassest motive
— pure, unashamed malice. And they will keep
making innuendoes about what women can do to
men. Man versus Woman. It's their constant
theme. It never lets up.

THE PASTOR has risen.

Can't you stay for supper? It's not much but you're
certainly welcome. I'm expecting the new doctor to
drop by. We can all dine together. Have you seen
him?

PASTOR: Just a glimpse. On my way down. He looks
a regular sort of chap.

CAPTAIN: Maybe I can get him on my side. You
never know. Oh, come on, do stay.

PASTOR: I'm sorry. I promised to be home in good
time for supper and my wife gets quite concerned
if I'm late.

CAPTAIN: Concerned! Furious you mean. Well, as
you like. *(helps him with coat)*

PASTOR: Now take care of yourself, Adolf. You're
looking a bit anxious; a bit under the weather.

CAPTAIN: Do you think so?

PASTOR: Well — not quite your old self, are you?

CAPTAIN: Laura's obviously got to you. For twenty
    years she'd been treating me as if I were a candidate
    for the funeral parlor.

PASTOR: Well, anyway. Take care. *(suddenly stops)*
    But what about this confirmation business?

CAPTAIN: That will have to work itself out. Don't
    worry your conscience over it. I certainly don't
    intend to martyr myself over it. But we've been all
    through that. Remember me to your wife.

PASTOR: Goodbye, Adolf. Give my best to Laura.

CAPTAIN turns to desk and begins examining bills.

*THE PASTOR encounters LAURA just before he
exits. She is wearing a long, flowing garment and has
obviously just risen. Their eyes meet and THE
PASTOR slowly nods his head as if to suggest he
hasn't been able to budge THE CAPTAIN. He then
goes and LAURA sidles into the room and over to
THE CAPTAIN who is lost in bookkeeping.*

LAURA: Could I . . .

CAPTAIN: *(turned away)* Just a second. Sixty-six,
    seventy-one, eighty-four, eighty-nine, ninety-two,
    one hundred. *(stops)* Well?

LAURA: Is it not convenient . . .?

CAPTAIN: The housekeeping!

LAURA: Um.

CAPTAIN: Leave me your bills and I'll check them.

LAURA: Bills?

CAPTAIN: Yes, bills.

LAURA: Do you expect me to keep bills?

CAPTAIN: Of course I expect you to keep bills.
We're in a precarious situation financially and
should it become necessary, I will have to furnish
strict accounts. Otherwise I shall be accused of
negligence.

LAURA: It's not my fault we're in a 'precarious
situation'.

CAPTAIN: Which is precisely what the accounts will
prove.

LAURA: It's not my fault our tenant-farmer refuses to
pay his rent.

CAPTAIN: Why recommend such a good-for-
nothing?

LAURA: Why accept such a good-for-nothing?

CAPTAIN: Because I wasn't allowed to eat in peace,
sleep in peace or work in peace until I'd taken him
on. You wanted him because your brother wanted
shot of him. Your mother wanted him because I
didn't. The governess wanted him because he was
a Methodist, and old Margaret wanted him because
she'd known his grandmother as a child. That is
why we took him, and if I hadn't, I'd be in a lunatic
asylum by now or reposing in the family vault.
However, there is your housekeeping and personal
allowance. You can hand in the accounts later.

Hands her four bills, hesitates, retrieves one and locks it into desk-drawer. Then takes ledger, crosses to easy chair to continue adding up.

LAURA: And do you keep account of all your private expenses?

CAPTAIN: That's not your concern.

LAURA: Of course not. Neither is my child's upbringing. I suppose after your great conference, all the necessary decisions have been made.

CAPTAIN: My decision was made a long time ago. I merely conveyed it to the only friend I have in the family. Bertha is to live in town. She'll leave here within fourteen days.

LAURA: *(after a beat)* With whom will she live, if I may ask?

CAPTAIN: Saevberg the solicitor.

LAURA: That Freethinker!

CAPTAIN: According to the law, a child is to be brought up in the father's faith.

LAURA: And the mother has no rights?

CAPTAIN: None whatsoever. According to the law, she surrenders her rights and her possessions to her husband. In return, she and her children receive his support.

LAURA: So, I'm to have no rights over my own child?

CAPTAIN: None. Once you've sold something you don't expect to get it back, and the money as well.

LAURA: But supposing the father and mother were to decide such matters between them?

CAPTAIN: How can that be? I want her in town. You want her at home. A compromise would have her living at the railway station between both points. Not a very satisfactory solution, I'm sure you'll agree.

LAURA: *(regards him quietly for a moment)* What was Nojd doing here?

CAPTAIN: That I'm afraid is a military secret.

LAURA: Which is known to the entire kitchen-staff.

CAPTAIN: Then doubtless you know it as well.

LAURA: I do.

CAPTAIN: And have passed judgement?

LAURA: The law does that.

CAPTAIN: The law does not know who the child's father is.

LAURA: People know that for themselves.

CAPTAIN: Discerning people contend that is something that can never be known with certainty.

LAURA: Really! Not to be able to tell a child's father!?

CAPTAIN: So they say.

LAURA: Then how is the father entitled to those rights over the mother's child?

LAURA: He acquires them when he takes on responsibility for the child — or has it thrust upon him. In marriage, of course, the question of paternity is not relevant.

LAURA: Isn't it?

CAPTAIN: I should hope not.

LAURA: And if the wife's been unfaithful?

CAPTAIN: That has no bearing on the present issue. *(closes ledger impatiently)* Is there anything else you'd like to know? *(beat)* In that case, I shall go to my room. Please let me know when the doctor arrives. *(stops)* The *moment* he arrives. One doesn't want to be discourteous, you understand?

LAURA: Perfectly.

THE CAPTAIN exits.

LAURA crumples the banknotes in her hands and reflects.

GRANDMOTHER: *(off-stage)* Laura!

LAURA: Yes?

GRANDMOTHER: Is my tea ready?

LAURA: Just coming.

BERTHA enters hurriedly. Looks expectanly at her mother for some news of her fate. LAURA nods almost imperceptibly then stretches out her arms towards her daughter. BERTHA moves into LAURA's embrace.

GRANDMOTHER: *(off-stage)* Laura! Laura!

LAURA tightens her grasp on BERTHA, her face hard and set.

Lights fade out.

Lights up.

DR. OESTERMARK standing alone.

After a moment, LAURA enters, stops, sizes him up and then adjusting her mask, walks resolutely towards him.

LAURA: Welcome, Doctor. The Captain is out for the moment, but I expect him back shortly.

DOCTOR: I'm so sorry I'm so late. I had to make a few calls on the way.

LAURA: Do sit down.

DOCTOR: Thank you.

LAURA: There's a lot of illness about just now. I do hope you'll manage. Living in a remote country district like this, it means so much to have a doctor who takes a real interest. And I've heard so many compliments paid you, I'm sure we shall become fast friends.

DOCTOR: That's very kind. I hope, however, for your sake, that my visits here will not be of a professional nature. I take it your own family enjoys good health . . .

LAURA: We've not been troubled by serious illness, I'm happy to say. Still . . . things aren't quite what they might be.

DOCTOR: Oh?

LAURA: Not all we would wish.

DOCTOR: That sounds a bit alarming.

LAURA: There are certain matters, personal things it's sometimes difficult to discuss.

DOCTOR: Surely not with one's doctor.

LAURA: No. Precisely. *(beat)* It's probably better to get all this out in the open from the start.

DOCTOR: Should we perhaps not defer our discussion until I've had the honor of meeting the Captain?

LAURA: That is the point, Doctor. You must hear this before you meet him.

DOCTOR: Does it concern him then?

LAURA: Yes — my poor, dear husband.

DOCTOR: Whatever the problem, madame, I can assure you that you can confide in me.

LAURA: My husband's mind is affected. You'll soon
           see for yourself.

DOCTOR: *(beat)* That's quite astonishing. I have
           read and admired the Captain's treatise on
           mineralogy in which he exhibits a clear and
           powerful intellect.

LAURA: I shall be overjoyed, Doctor, if we turn out
           to be mistaken.

DOCTOR: It's entirely possible of course, that his
           judgement may be impaired in other ways. What
           precisely . . . ?

LAURA: That's just what we're afraid of. You see,
           sometimes he has the most extraordinary ideas. Of
           course, it's common for scholars to be eccentric
           and difficult, but this has got entirely out of hand.
           For instance, he has a positive mania for buying
           things.

DOCTOR: What kind of things?

LAURA: Books. Crates of them. Which he never
           reads.

DOCTOR: It's not unusual for a scholar to collect
           books.

LAURA: Are you saying I am lying?

DOCTOR: Not at all. I'm sure *you* believe what
           you're telling me, it's only that . . .

LAURA: Is it normal for a man to claim he can see
           what is happening on other planets — in a

microscope?

DOCTOR: Does he claim that?

LAURA: Yes.

DOCTOR: In a microscope?

LAURA: In a microscope!

DOCTOR: If that is true, it would certainly suggest . . .

LAURA: *If* it is true! Do you think I am standing here making up stories. I'm telling you the most intimate details of our family life.

DOCTOR: My dear lady, I'm honored that you feel able to confide in me. But you understand, as a doctor, I'm obliged to investigate the matter thoroughly before venturing an opinion. Does the Captain show signs of instability or vacillation?

LAURA: Signs! We've been married twenty years and he has never yet taken a decision without immediately changing his mind.

DOCTOR: Is he very inflexible?

LAURA: He always insists on having his own way, and no sooner does he get it then he loses interest and asks me to decide.

DOCTOR: That is significant. It obviously needs careful examination. The will, you see, is like the backbone of the mind. If *it* is impaired, the entire mind can be affected.

LAURA: God knows I've tried to keep peace through all these long, trying years. If you knew what I have been through Doctor; if you only knew.

DOCTOR: I'm very distressed to hear all of this, and I assure you I'll do everything in my power to help. But I must have your assistance. You must avoid touching on any subject that might provoke your husband. In a troubled mind, fancies grow like mushrooms and can easily develop into an obsession. You understand?

LAURA: I mustn't make him suspicious.

DOCTOR: Exactly. A person with a troubled mind is highly impressionable and apt to believe almost anything.

LAURA: I see, Doctor.

DOCTOR: But don't fret, We'll do everything we can and I'm sure things will turn out all right.

LAURA: *(taking his hand)* Thank you, Doctor.

She allows her hand to linger in his for a moment.

Fade-out.

Lights up. THE DOCTOR.

GRANDMOTHER: *(off-stage)* Laura! Laura! *(DOCTOR turns towards GRANDMOTHER's voice as CAPTAIN enters from opposite side)*

DOCTOR: *(shaking his hand)* It's a great honor to make the acquaintance of such a distinguished scientist.

CAPTAIN: Rubbish! In the army one cannot immerse oneself in research. There are so many other things to bother about. Still, I do believe I'm on the brink of a rather interesting discovery.

DOCTOR: Oh?

CAPTAIN: I've been using spectrum-analysis to examine certain meteoric stones and I've discoverd signs of coal — a clear indication of organic life. What do you say to that?

DOCTOR: And you can see that through a microscope?

CAPTAIN: Microscope? Good God, no! A spectrascope.

DOCTOR: *(taken aback)* Spectrascope. Of course. How stupid of me. Well. I suppose before long you'll be able to tell us what's happening on Jupiter.

CAPTAIN: Not what *is* happening, but what *has* happened. *(studies DOCTOR quizzically)* but dammit all, I'm still waiting for books ordered from Paris months ago. I really believe all the bookshops in Europe have conspired against me. Not one of them has acknowledged my requests. I've sent abusive letters, even telegrams — all to no avail. It's just infuriating!

DOCTOR: Normal inefficiency, I expect.

CAPTAIN: But I'll never be able to finish my thesis in time. There's some chap in Berlin working on the self-same subject . . . Still, that's neither here nor there. What we ought to be discussing is your accommodations. If you prefer to live on the grounds, we can put you up in a little flat in the upper wing. Or you could have the old Doctor's quarters.

DOCTOR: Just as you like.

CAPTAIN: No, as *you* like. Just say which.

DOCTOR: It's really up to you, Captain.

CAPTAIN: State your preference, Doctor. It makes no difference to me.

DOCTOR: Well really, I can't . . .

CAPTAIN: For Christ's sake, man, make up your mind! Are you such a dunce you don't know where you want to live? Now choose before I really lose my temper.

DOCTOR: If it's up to me then, I should prefer to live here.

CAPTAIN: *(mellowing)* Thank God that's done. You must forgive me, Doctor, but nothing irritates me more than people who say they don't care one way or the other. *(rings)* Margaret!

MARGARET enters.

Is the upstairs room made up?

NURSE: Yes, it's all ready.

CAPTAIN: Good. Then I won't keep you any longer, Doctor. I expect you want to get some rest. We'll talk tomorrow.

DOCTOR: Goodnight, Captain.

CAPTAIN: I expect my wife has put you in the picture — told you how the land lies.

DOCTOR: She did tell me one or two things she thought it might be useful for me to know. Goodnight, Captain. *(Exists)*

CAPTAIN: *(irritably)* Well, what do you want?

NURSE: Now listen Adolf, dear.

CAPTAIN: Go on, talk Margaret, You're about the only person I can bear around here.

NURSE: Why can't you come to some kind of compromise over the child? She is her mother, after all.

CAPTAIN: And I'm her father.

NURSE: Now, now, now. A father has lots of other things to concern himself with, but a mother has nothing but her child.

CAPTAIN: Exactly. She has only one responsibility while I have three — including hers. Do you think I'd have stuck it out in places like this all my life if I hadn't had to support both of them?

NURSE: I wasn't talking about that.

CAPTAIN: No, I'm sure you weren't. You just want to put me in the wrong again.

NURSE: I want what's best for you. You know that.

CAPTAIN: But you don't know what *is* best for me. Don't you see, it's not enough just giving the child life? I want to give her my soul as well.

NURSE: Well, I can't follow all that, but I still think you ought to come to some understanding with the mistress.

CAPTAIN: You've turned against me as well.

NURSE: How can you say such a thing? How could I ever turn against my little baby?

CAPTAIN: You *have* been like a mother to me, it's true. Stood by me against all the others, but now, when I really need you, you desert and go over to the enemy.

NURSE: Enemy?

CAPTAIN: Yes, enemy! You know what it's like living in this house. You've seen it all — from the beginning.

NURSE: Dear God, why must you torture each other all the time? People who are so good and kind to everyone else. The mistress is never like that to me or anyone else.

CAPTAIN: Only me, I know it quite well. But I'm telling you, Margaret, if you desert me now, you will regret it for the rest of your life. There's some plot being hatched here. I can feel it. And that doctor is no friend, I'm sure of that.

NURSE: Oh Adolf, you always think the worst of everyone, but that's because you never found the True Faith. That's your trouble really.

CAPTAIN: And you *have* found 'the True Faith', have you? You and your confounded Baptists. How fortunate.

NURSE: More fortunate than you, Adolf. And happier. Humble your heart and you shall soon see how God will shed his grace and bring love to your neighbor.

CAPTAIN: Isn't it curious — as soon as you mention God and grace, your voice becomes hard and your eyes glow with hatred. Those are the signs, are they, of the true faith?

NURSE: All your learning has made you proud, but it won't be any help to you when you stand before the Greatest Judge of All.

CAPTAIN: What do dumb creatures like you know about 'my learning'?

NURSE: Shame, shame, Adolf — the things you say. But never mind, old Margaret loves her great little boy and when he's in trouble, he'll creep right back to her like the good little boy he really is.

CAPTAIN: I'm sorry, Margaret. I know you're the only one in this house I can trust. Help me. I feel something terrible is going to happen.

NURSE: *(comforting him)* There, there, big little
     baby. *(hugs him)*

> *There is a bloodcurdling scream from without. THE*
> *CAPTAIN abruptly draws out of THE NURSE's*
> *embrace. They look at each other in astonishment*
> *and dread.*

> *The lights fade out.*

> *Lights up.*

> *THE NURSE is gone, BERTHA comes running into*
> *THE CAPTAIN's arms.*

CAPTAIN: What is it, what is it?

BERTHA: It's Grandmama, she wants to hit me.

CAPTAIN: Hit you?

BERTHA: All I did was play a little trick on her.

CAPTAIN: What's happened?

BERTHA: You mustn't tell. Promise.

CAPTAIN: Yes, yes. What is it?

BERTHA: *(taking THE CAPTAIN downstage, away*
     from the threat of GRANDMOTHER) In the
     evenings, she sits me down at the table, turns the
     lamp down very low and puts this pen into my
     hands.

CAPTAIN: And?

BERTHA: Then she commands the spirits to write.

CAPTAIN: *(beat)* I'll be damned. Why haven't you said something about this before?

BERTHA: I didn't dare. Grandma says the spirits take revenge if anyone talks about them.

CAPTAIN: And what happens then — when you're sitting with the pen?

BERTHA: It writes, but I can't tell if I'm doing it or they are. Sometimes it goes well. Other times nothing happens at all. When I'm tired, for instance. But I have to make something happen all the same for her sake, and tonight, it was going well, but then Grandma read it over and said all I'd done was copy down an old poem and she was just furious. *(starts to cry)*

CAPTAIN: *(comforting)* Now, now, now. Tell me. Do you believe there are such things as spirtis?

BERTHA: I don't know.

CAPTAIN: I know there aren't.

BERTHA: But you do worse things. Grandma says you look into other planets.

CAPTAIN: Does she? And what else does Grandma say?

BERTHA: That you can work magic.

CAPTAIN: She lies then.

BERTHA:.   Grandmother doesn't lie.

CAPTAIN: How do you know?

BERTHA: Then mother does too. *(pause)* If you say mother lies, I'll never believe a word you say ever again!

CAPTAIN: Now I haven't said that, and so you must believe what I'm going to tell you. For your own good, for the sake of your future, you must leave this house. You'd like to live in town wouldn't you, and learn something useful?

BERTHA: Oh, I'd love to live in town — anything to get away from here. As long as I could see you sometimes — often. It's so dreary here, like an endless winter night — but when you come home, it's like a spring morning when they take down the shutters and the windows are thrown wide open.

CAPTAIN: My darling, my darling.

BERTHA: *(extricating herself)* But you must be nice to mother. You mustn't make her cry.

CAPTAIN: So you *would* like to live in town?

BERTHA: Oh yes.

CAPTAIN: But suppose your mother doesn't want you to?

BERTHA: She must.

CAPTAIN: And if not?

BERTHA: Then I don't know . . . but she must.

CAPTAIN: Will you ask her?

BERTHA: She doesn't take any notice of me. You ask her.

CAPTAIN: But if you want it and I want it, and she doesn't, what then?

BERTHA: Then it'll start all over again. Why can't you both . . .

LAURA has entered a moment before. BERTHA suddenly becomes aware of her, leaps from her FATHER's lap and stands downstage, facing away from both parents . . . as if invisible.

LAURA: Since it is Bertha's fate that's being decided, perhaps we can be allowed to hear her opinion.

CAPTAIN: The child can hardly be expected to have anything constructive to say about the development of young girls. We, on the other hand, have some experience on the subject and therefore are better qualified to judge.

LAURA: But as we cannot agree, it is surely for Bertha to cast the deciding vote.

CAPTAIN: I will not permit anyone to interfere with my rights — neither woman nor child. Bertha, leave us.

BERTHA hesitates and looks fearfully to LAURA.

Leave us, I said!

She exits hurriedly.

LAURA: You were afraid to let her speak because you knew she'd be on my side.

CAPTAIN: I know she wants to leave home, but I also know you have the power to make her change her mind.

LAURA: Oh, am I so powerful?

CAPTAIN: Diabolically so. You have a fiendish power for getting your own way. And you are thoroughly unscrupulous about the means you use. For example, how did you manage to get rid of Dr. Norling and replace him with this new man?

LAURA: You tell me.

CAPTAIN: You insulted the old doctor so relentlessly he had no choice but to go. Then you got your brother to canvass for this new man.

LAURA: *(refusing to pursue the subject)* Is Bertha to leave then?

CAPTAIN: Within fourteen days.

LAURA: Is that final?

CAPTAIN: It is.

LAURA: I shall prevent it.

CAPTAIN: I'm afraid you can't.

LAURA: Do you think I will allow my daughter to be

taught by godless people that all she has learned from her mother is nonsense? To turn my own daughter against me?

CAPTAIN: And do you think I will allow ignorant and conceited women to teach my daughter that her father is a charlatan?

LAURA: That shouldn't matter so much to you — now.

CAPTAIN: What do you mean by that?

LAURA: Since a mother is closer to her child and since no one can be certain who a child's father really is.

CAPTAIN: What has that got to do with it?

LAURA: You don't know if you are Bertha's father.

CAPTAIN: Don't know?

LAURA: No one *can* know for sure, can they?

CAPTAIN: Is this some sort of joke?

LAURA: I am simply applying your own theory. How do you know I haven't been unfaithful to you?

CAPTAIN: I can believe a lot about you, but not that. And if it were true, it would be the last thing you would talk about.

LAURA: Suppose I was ready to endure anything, being turned out, ostracized, despised, anything, rather than lose my child? Suppose I am telling the truth when I say Bertha is my child — but not yours. Suppose . . .

CAPTAIN: Stop it.

LAURA: Your 'rights' would vanish.

CAPTAIN: Not unless you could *prove* I wasn't the father.

LAURA: Would that be so difficult? Would you like me to?

CAPTAIN: Stop this right now!

LAURA: It would simply be a matter of giving you the name of the true father, the time, the place. When was Bertha born? Three years after the marriage, right? That would mean . . .

CAPTAIN: Stop it or . . .

LAURA: *(after a beat)* Or what?

THE CAPTAIN is impotent with rage; LAURA stares him down.

Very well. We'll drop the matter. But think carefully before you decide to send Bertha away. You don't want to make yourself look ridiculous.

CAPTAIN: *(beat)* I could almost weep.

LAURA: That would make you even more ridiculous.

CAPTAIN: But never you.

LAURA: No, we're in a somewhat stronger position.

CAPTAIN: Which is why we cannot attack you.

LAURA: Why attack a superior enemy?

GRANDMOTHER: Superior?

LAURA: Yes, it's quite curious, but I've never met any man without feeling I was his superior.

CAPTAIN: Well, now you've met your match and I'll see that you never forget it.

LAURA: That should be interesting.

NURSE: *(entering)* Dinner's ready. Come along.

THE CAPTAIN smoulders at LAURA for a moment then briskly moves to his chair. THE NURSE immediately senses the atmosphere.

LAURA: Aren't you going to have dinner?

CAPTAIN: No thank you.

LAURA: Are you going to sulk?

CAPTAIN: I'm not hungry.

LAURA: Do come along. Everyone will start asking questions. Be a good boy and come along. *(beat)* Very well then. Suit yourself. *(exits)*

NURSE: Now, what's all that about?

CAPTAIN: Can you tell me Margaret, why it is that

makes women think they can treat grown men as if
they were helpless children?

NURSE: Don't ask me. I suppose you're all born of
women — whether children or grown men.

CAPTAIN: While no woman is born of man. Tell me
Margaret, you believe I am Bertha's father, don't
you?

NURSE: Lord what a silly boy you are! Of course
you're the father of your own child. What kind of
question is that? Now come along and stop sulking.
That's a good boy.

CAPTAIN: *(seeing THE NURSE as if transformed
into a witch)* Get away. Don't touch me. Go back
to Hell with all the rest of your demons!

NURSE: Now listen, Adolf . .

CAPTAIN: Get away, I say! *(cringes and retreats from
THE NURSE)* Svaerd, Svaerd! Harness the sleigh.
Quick! Quick!

NURSE: God help us, what's brought on all this!

CAPTAIN: *(off-stage)* And don't expect me back
before midnight!

*BERTHA hearing the racket, rushes in to discover a
distressed NURSE, after a moment, LAURA strides
in entirely composed, BERTHA and THE NURSE
turn to her.*

LAURA: Shall we finish our dinner.

Fade out.

*Sound of thunder and rainstorm. The lamp on the
CAPTAIN's desk begins to glow in the darkness
while the storm rages without. Its light increases in
intensity to a blinding glow then gradually subsides
and fades out. When the lights next come up, THE
CAPTAIN is sitting upstage, his arms wrapped
around himself as if wearing a straitjacket. He looks
straight ahead and what he sees is . . . THE
DOCTOR and LAURA appearing from opposite
sides.*

DOCTOR: I am by no means convinced by your
    diagnosis. First of all, you were quite mistaken in
    saying he had reached his conclusions about other
    planets with the aid of a microscope. Now that I
    have learned it was a spectroscope, not only is
    there no indication of mental derangement, but it is
    quite possible he has made a significant contribution
    to science.

LAURA: But I didn't say that.

DOCTOR: I have a written record of our conversation,
    madame, and I remember I questioned you quite
    particularly on this point. One must be scrupulously
    accurate in making accusations which might lead
    to a man being certified.

LAURA: *(slowly)* Certified?

The lights slowly turn red.

*A change appears to take place in THE DOCTOR's
and LAURA's formal relationship. They move
slowly, and with a new relaxation, to two easy*

*chairs. Their manner now suggests the intimacy of
lovers. Upstage, THE CAPTAIN sits motionless
watching the scene.*

DOCTOR: *(insinuatingly)* I assume you realize that if
a person is certified insane, he loses all civil and
family rights.

LAURA: *(smiling)* Really, I didn't know that.

DOCTOR: *(sharing LAURA's smile)* The Captain
spoke of not getting any replies from his booksellers.
May I ask whether, from the best of intentions of
course, you have intercepted his correspondence?

LAURA: *(not defensive)* It is my duty to protect the
family. I couldn't let him ruin us and do nothing
about it.

DOCTOR: I wonder if you quite realize the
consequences of such actions. If he were to discover
you've been interfering in his affairs, his suspicions
would be confirmed and he might develop a
persecution mania. Particularly as by thwarting his
will, you have already put a sizeable pressure upon
him. Surely you must realize how infuriating it is to
have one's deepest desires frustrated?

LAURA: Do I not?

DOCTOR: Then imagine how he must feel.

*THE DOCTOR has approached LAURA. He now
extends his hand to her, she rises — very close to
him — and he takes her in his arms. They kiss
intensely until LAURA, growing more and more
excited, breaks out of the embrace and crosses away.*

LAURA: It's well past midnight, and he's still not
           back. We must be ready for the worst.

DOCTOR: *(following close)* Tell me what happened
           this evening — after I left.

LAURA: He talked in the wildest way and said the
           most incredible things. Can you imagine, he asked
           if he was really his own child's father.

DOCTOR: Where did he get that idea?

LAURA: He'd been questioning one of the men about
           some girl who was having a child, and when I took
           the girl's side, he became incensed and said no one
           could ever be sure who was any child's father. I did
           everything I could to calm him down, but it's all
           become too much for me. *(cries)*

DOCTOR: *(comforting)* Has he had these delusions
           before?

LAURA: Six years ago, it was very much the same
           kind of thing. Then he actually admitted — in a
           letter to his doctor — that he feared his mind
           might be going.

DOCTOR: I can stay if you like, until he gets back. I
           could say your mother was not feeling well and I
           had to see to her. That would allay any suspicions.

LAURA: *(clinging to him)* Oh, please don't leave us.
           If you only knew how difficult it is for me — for all
           of us.

           *They kiss and gradually return to their former
           positions. The relationship returns to its formal*

nature and the red lighting disappears.

(formally) Wouldn't it be better to tell him straight out the truth of his condition?

DOCTOR: *(formally)* One must never do that with mentally disturbed patients, unless they themselves bring up the subject and even then, with the greatest delicacy. It all depends on how things develop. But in any case, we mustn't be found together. It would look less suspicious if I was in the other room.

LAURA: Margaret can wait in here. She always waits up for him when he goes out. *(calling)* Margaret! Margaret! Come along, Doctor.

She moves out hurriedly with THE DOCTOR following.

The thunderstorm crackles in the background.

The light on THE CAPTAIN burns bright.

The lamps again begin to glow and gradually increase in intensity until it is a blinding light. Then it slowly fades down and out. In the darkness, THE NURSE sits.

The light on THE CAPTAIN remains constant and the lights downstage return.

THE NURSE, dozing in an easy chair.

BERTHA: *(entering)* Can I sit with you? It's so dismal upstairs.

NURSE: Goodness, Bertha. Aren't you asleep yet?

BERTHA: I can't sleep. And besides, I've got to finish father's Christmas present. You see.

She pulls off a black covering from an object she has brought with her. When it is removed, it reveals a small effigy costumed like THE CAPTAIN. As BERTHA holds it up before THE NURSE the red lighting gradually returns.

And look, I've got something for you as well.

She moves to THE NURSE's seat and hands her two long needles — like hatpins, retaining two for herself.

NURSE: *(pretending to admonish; with a sly smile on her face)* But it's already gone midnight and you've got to get up early in the morning.

BERTHA: I can't sit up there alone. I'm sure there are ghosts.

Thrusts needle into effigy's heart.

NURSE: *(feigning shock)* Ghosts, what did I tell you? Mark my word, there's no guardian angel hovering over this house. *(thrusts needle into effigy)* Tell me what you heard, Bertha.

BERTHA: *(feigning)* Singing. Up in the attic.

NURSE: In the attic. At this time of night.

BERTHA: *(feigning)* Such a sad song. I've never heard anything like it. It seemed to be coming from the closet, where the cradle is.

NURSE: And such a dreadful night too. It sounds like the chimneys will blow down. 'Alas, what is this earthly life? Sorrow, trouble, grief and pain. Even when it seems most fair, misery returns again.' *(thrusts a needle into the effigy)* God grant we have a happy Christmas.

BERTHA: *(slyly)* Is father really ill?

NURSE: Of course he is, child.

BERTHA: Then he won't be coming to our Christmas party, will he? *(They both smile conspiratorially)* Why doesn't he stay in bed if he's ill?

NURSE: Staying in bed doesn't help his kind of illness dear.

BERTHA: And why is that? *(thrusts needle into effigy's head)*

The red lights slowly fade away leaving normal lighting.

NURSE: *(hugging her)* Hush, hush, you ask too many questions. Go to bed now, or the master will be angry.

BERTHA, restored to her normal state, recovers the effigy and exits.

Lights come to full as THE CAPTAIN rises from his seat up stage and staggers into the scene proper. He is clearly drunk.

CAPTAIN: Still up, are you? Go to bed.

NURSE: I only waited until you . . .

THE CAPTAIN sits heavily at desk and begins examining photo-album.

Adolf . . .

CAPTAIN: What now?

NURSE: The old lady is sick. The doctor's had to be called.

CAPTAIN: Is it serious?

NURSE: Just a little chill I think.

CAPTAIN: Margaret, who was the father of your child?

NURSE: I've told you a thousand times, Johannson, that layabout.

CAPTAIN: But are you sure?

NURSE: Of course I'm sure. He was the only one.

CAPTAIN: But was *he* sure he was the only one? No, because he couldn't be. You can of course. That's the difference, isn't it?

NURSE: What difference?

CAPTAIN   You can't see it, of course, but there is a difference nevertheless. *(checking photo-album, removes photo of BERTHA)* Do you think Bertha looks like me?

NURSE: You're like two peas in a pod.

CAPTAIN: Did Johannson admit he was the father?

NURSE: He had to.

CAPTAIN: *(shutting the photo album)* Horrible, horrible. *(senses THE DOCTOR's presence)* How is the old lady then?

DOCTOR: Nothing serious. A sprained ankle.

CAPTAIN: Laura said she had a chill. Appears to be conflicting diagnoses.

DOCTOR looks awkwardly to THE NURSE who looks guilty and exits.

Is is true, Doctor, that if you cross a zebra with a mare you get striped foals?

DOCTOR: *(wary)* Yes.

CAPTAIN: And is it not also true that the foals may continue to be striped even if it then gets crossed with a stallion?

DOCTOR: Yes, that is also true.

CAPTAIN: Therefore in certain circumstances, a black stallion can sire a striped foal and vice verse?

DOCTOR: That would appear to be the case.

CAPTAIN: Therefore, a child's resemblance to his

father is almost wholly irrelevant.

DOCTOR:　Well . . .

CAPTAIN:　And so it follows that the identity of a
child's father can never be proved conclusively.
You're a widower, I believe. Have you had any
children?

DOCTOR:　Yes.

CAPTAIN:　Didn't you feel somewhat ridiculous
playing the father's role? Is there anything more
absurd, I ask myself, than a father trotting down
the street with a child at his side. Referring to 'his
children'? 'My wife's children' is what he should
say. Did you never consider the false position you
were in? Did you never experience any doubts? I
won't say suspicions for, as a gentleman, I assume
your wife was above suspicion.

DOCTOR:　No, I did not, Captain, and isn't it Goethe
who has written: 'A man must take his children on
trust.'

CAPTAIN:　Trust! Where a woman is concerned?

DOCTOR:　There are women and women.

CAPTAIN:　My own experience leads me to believe
there's only one kind. When I was a young man
and, even if I do say so myself, a handsome one, I
had two experiences which gave me pause. The
first was on a steamer. I was in the lounge with
some friends and the young waitress told us, with
tears streaming down her face, how her lover had
been drowned at sea. I sympathized of course, and

ordered champagne to try to cheer her up. After
the second glass, I touched her knee, after the
fourth, her thigh and before morning, I had
consoled her entirely.

DOCTOR: One swallow doesn't make a summer.

CAPTAIN: No, but two snowstorms do make a
winter. My second experience was even more
edifying. I was spending some time in Lysekil
where I got to know a young married woman who
had come there with her children, her husband
having remained in town. She was highly religious;
very strict principles, read me moral lectures,
preached sermons to me. The picture of virtue. I
loaned her a couple of books as she showed some
interest in them and when it came time to say
farewell she actually returned them. Three months
later, I found inside one of those books a visiting
card containing a fairly explicit declaration of love.
Oh, it was innocent, as innocent as a declaration of
love can be coming from a married woman and
addressed to a man who was virtually a stranger
and who had never given her any encouragement
whatsoever.
Moral: Never trust any human being too much.

DOCTOR: Nor too little.

CAPTAIN: Exactly. Just so much and no more. But
you see, Doctor, that woman was so heedlessly
treacherous that she allowed her husband to
believe she'd developed a passion for me. That's
the horror of it, Doctor. They don't seem to realize
their potential for creating evil. That may mitigate
their crimes somewhat, but it doesn't remove their
guilt. *(freeze as LAURA enters slowly and stands*

motionless upstage)

DOCTOR: These are morbid thoughts and you
     should guard against them. It's unhealthy to . . .

CAPTAIN: Don't lecture me about health, Doctor.
     All steam-boilers explode when the pressure-gauge
     reaches the limit, but the limit isn't the same in
     every case. Each has its own breaking point.
     Nevertheless, you are here to keep watch on me. I
     know that very well. If I were not a man, I might
     have the right to accuse, or, as you might say, air
     my grievance. Then I might be able to give you a
     complete diagnosis of my illness and what is more
     to the point, its history. But being a man, only a
     man, I must, like the noble Roman, fold my arms
     across my breast and hold my peace until I die.
     (beat. THE DOCTOR begins to object) Goodnight,
     Doctor.

DOCTOR: If you are ill, Captain — or believe that
     you are, it is no reflection on your honor as a man
     to tell me the truth. It is only right and proper that
     I hear both sides.

CAPTAIN: I would have thought you'd be quite
     satisfied with only one side.

DOCTOR: You're wrong. And I should tell you
     Captain, when I go to the theater and hear Mrs.
     Alving blackening the memory of her dead husband,
     I always think what a damned shame it is the fellow
     is dead and cannot defend himself.

CAPTAIN: Do you think he'd have dared open his
     mouth if he *had* been alive? If any husband rose
     from the grave to tell his side of the story, do you

really think he'd be listened to? Goodnight, Doctor. Don't fret. I'm perfectly calm. It's quite safe for you to go to bed.

DOCTOR: Goodnight then, Captain. I shall not concern myself any further with this matter.

CAPTAIN: Are we enemies?

DOCTOR: Not at all. It's just a shame we seem unable to be friends.

THE DOCTOR exits.

THE CAPTAIN stirs in his seat and visibly sobers up. Up stage LAURA who has entered earlier and stood motionless, stirs to life.

The light increases to full.

CAPTAIN: *(without looking at her)* Although it's very late, we'd better have things out now.

Slowly, LAURA moves from up stage to her easy chair and sits.

CAPTAIN: This evening I went to the Post Office and collected the letters. It is clear that you have been intercepting my correspondence. As a result of losing all this time, my project is virtually destroyed and my expectations shattered.

LAURA: I acted out of the best intentions. You were neglecting your military duties because of this other work.

CAPTAIN: *(sarcastically)* 'Best intentions'. You knew

very well that one day I would win more distinction
in this field than I ever could in the army, and your
'intentions' were to prevent my winning laurels of
any kind as this would only emphasise your own
inferiority. *(beat)* Now it has been my turn to
intercept your letters.

LAURA: How chivalrous.

CAPTAIN: Entirely in keeping with the high opinion
you have of me. It is clear from these letters that
for some time now you have been turning my
friends against me and spreading rumors about
my mental state. And you've been quite successful
for there is now hardly anyone, from the Colonel to
the cook, who believes I am sane. But the truth of
my condition is this: my reason, as you well know,
is entirely unaffected. I can perform my professional
duties *and* my duties as a father. My emotions are
still, more or less, under control and my will-power
remains intact. Despite the fact that you have been
chipping away at it, day after day, hour after hour.
I won't appeal to your feelings. You haven't any.
Instead, I shall appeal to your own self-interest.

LAURA: Go on.

CAPTAIN: As a result of your behavior, you have
sewn doubts in my mind. My judgement is unsteady
and my thoughts not as lucid as they have been.
The insanity you have so lovingly fostered may well
be on its way. What you now have to decide is
whether it would be to your advantage for me to be
well or ill. Just consider. If I suffer a total collapse,
I shall be removed from the army and you will be
without support. If I die, the insurance will come
straight to you, but if I take my own life, you will

get nothing. Therefore, it is to your advantage that
I live my life out.

LAURA: *(pause)* You would never take your own life.

CAPTAIN: Are you so certain of that? What is the
point of living when one has nothing and no one to
live for?

LAURA: *(after a pause)* Then you give in?

CAPTAIN: No. I propose a truce.

LAURA: Its conditions?

CAPTAIN: *(with difficulty)* That I am allowed to
retain my reason. Remove my doubts and I will
give up the fight.

LAURA: About what?

CAPTAIN: Bertha.

LAURA: Do you have doubts?

CAPTAIN: Yes, and you know very well it was you
who planted them.

LAURA: I?

CAPTAIN: You loosed them like henbane into my
ear and encouraged them to grow. Free me from
this uncertainty. Tell me straight out, 'This is the
truth. This is how it happened', and I will forgive
you in advance.

LAURA: *(pause)* I can hardly plead guilty to a crime I

haven't committed.

CAPTAIN: What does it matter to you? You know very well I would never divulge a word of it. Do you think a man wants to go about proclaiming his own shame?

LAURA: If I say it isn't true, you still won't be sure. But if I say it is, you will be. Would you rather it were true?

CAPTAIN: Yes, I suppose I would. Because the one cannot be proved whereas the other can.

LAURA: I believe you'd actually like me to be guilty, so you can get rid of me and have absolute control over the child. But you can't trick me that easily.

CAPTAIN: If I knew you were guilty, do you think I would take on another man's child?

LAURA: I'm sure you wouldn't — which is why I know you were lying when you said you would forgive me in advance.

CAPTAIN: Laura, don't destroy me. You've got to understand what I'm saying. If the child is not rightfully mine, I have no rights over her and want none. But that is what you want, isn't it? *(LAURA turns her head away)* Oh, I see. You want more than that. You want power over the child with me still there to support you both!

LAURA: Power? Of course. What is all this constant struggle about if not power?

CAPTAIN: I don't believe in any life hereafter. This

child was my life after death. My chance for
immortality. The only one we ever have. Take her
from me and I'm left with nothing.

LAURA: We should have parted long ago.

CAPTAIN: The child kept us together, but the bond
became a chain. How did that happen? I've never
really considered it before, but now I recall all sorts
of things. Memories that accuse you; that condemn
you. It was two years into the marriage. Still we
had no children. You know best why. Then I was
ill. Feverish. Close to death. One day, when my
head was clear for a few moments, I heard voices in
the adjoining room. You and the lawyer. Discussing
property. Money. He was saying as there were no
children, you couldn't inherit. He asked if you
were expecting one. I couldn't make out what you
said. After some time I recovered. Then we had a
child. *(pause. He turns to her)* Who is the father?

LAURA: You.

CAPTAIN: I am not! There's a terrible crime buried
here and it's beginning to stink to high heaven.
You women were tenderhearted enough to free
your black slaves, but you kept your white ones! I
have worked and slaved for you and your child and
your family. Ruined my career. Abandoned all
hope of promotion. Been racked and tortured.
Endured sleepless nights worrying about your
future. My hair has turned grey so that you and
your child might live free from care. I've borne all
of this — without complaint — because I believed
I was the father of that child. That was the most
contemptible form of theft — the most unforgivable
slavery. I have served seventeen years hard labor

while being entirely innocent of any crime. How
can you make that up to me? How?

LAURA: (*quietly*) You really are mad.

CAPTAIN: That's what you hope, isn't it? And
what's more, I've seen you cover up your crime,
even sympathized with you. Lulled your guilty
conscience to sleep, thinking I was soothing away
your morbid thoughts. I've heard you cry out in
your sleep and refused to listen. The other night.
Bertha's birthday. About two or three in the
morning. I was up, reading. You screamed in your
sleep. 'Keep away! Keep away!', as if you were
being strangled, 'Don't come! Don't come!' I
slammed my fist against the wall. I didn't want to
hear any more. I'd had my suspicions for a long
time, but I didn't dare have them confirmed. All
this I have suffered for you. How can you make
that up to me. How?

LAURA: I swear to God and all that I hold sacred
that you are Bertha's father.

CAPTAIN: But you've already said a mother should
commit any crime for the sake of her child — so
why not a false vow? You're used to those, aren't
you? Laura, I beg of you, for the sake of the past, I
implore you as a wounded man begs to be put out
of his misery — tell me the truth! Can't you see
that I'm as helpless as a child, begging for pity as a
child begs to its mother. I'm no longer a grown
man — a soldier who issues commands. All I ask is
the pity you would extend to any wounded man. I
renounce every vestige of power I may have had,
and only beg for mercy — on my life.

LAURA: What? You, a man, in tears?

He weeps like a child, burying his head in her lap.

Weep, weep, my baby, and you shall have your
mother again to comfort you. Do you remember, it
was as a second mother that I first came into your
life. Your great strong body was frail. You were
like an overgrown baby come too soon into the
world, unwanted even.

CAPTAIN: It's true. My mother and father didn't
want me. I came against their will, and so, was
born without a will. When I took you in my arms, I
felt I was whole — for the first time. I let you rule
me completely. That's how you got the upper hand.
I, who on the field among my troops, blustered and
dominated, was with you docile and obedient. I
looked up to you, heeded your every word. Saw
you as a superior being and I, your foolish little
boy.

LAURA: And I loved you as if you were my little boy.
But didn't you see how, when your feelings changed
and you came to me as a lover, I was ashamed. The
joy I used to feel in your arms gave way to such
intense feelings of guilt, it was as if my very blood
had become tainted. You turned the mother into a
mistress — horrible!

CAPTAIN: I saw, but I didn't understand. I thought
it was my lack of virility you despised. I wanted to
prove myself to you as a man.

LAURA: That was a mistake. It was the mother that
was your friend. The woman was always your
enemy. Love between man and woman *is* war, but

don't think I just gave myself to you. I didn't. I took what I wanted. But you always had the upper hand. I knew that and I wanted you to know it too.

CAPTAIN: It was you who had the upper hand, not I. You always! You hypnotized me so that I could neither hear nor see, but only obey. You could give me a stone and make me believe it was a peach. You could persuade me that your silliest whims were brilliant strokes of genius. You had the power to corrupt me, make me do the shabbiest things. You never had any real intelligence yet, instead of being guided by me, you had your own way in everything. But then I shrugged off your spell, looked about me and saw that I'd lost my integrity. I wanted to redeem myself though some noble action, some feat, some discovery. If nothing else, an honorable suicide. I wanted to go to the wars, but there were none. It was then that I threw myself into science. And now, when I should be stretching out my hand to reap the rewards of my labor, you hack off my arm. Now I am entirely without honor and a man cannot live without that.

LAURA: And a woman . . .?

CAPTAIN: She has her children, but he hasn't. And because of that we went on living as if we *were* children, nourishing ourselves on fancies and illusions — and then we woke. With a start. All tangled up. Our feet where our head ought to be. Roused by someone who was himself a sleepwalker. When women grow so old they're no longer women they get beards on their chin. I wonder what happens to men when they grow so old, they're no longer men? We crowed proudly like cocks, but we were only capons, and the hens that answered

our calls, they were just as sexless as we. We
crowed to greet the dawn, but it wasn't dawn at all.
It was bright moonlight we'd mistaken for the
dawn, and we weren't heralding any new day, only
sitting amidst old ruins, at the end of our lives. It
hadn't even been a proper sleep. Only a little nap,
squirming with bad dreams. No sleep. No
awakening. *(pause)*

LAURA: You should have been a writer, you know.
But if you have any more fantasies, keep them till
tomorrow. It's very late.

CAPTAIN: Do you hate me?

LAURA: Sometimes. When you're a man.

CAPTAIN: If we are descended from the apes, as
they say, it must have been two very different
species. We just aren't of the same blood, are we?

LAURA: And what does that mean?

CAPTAIN: If it is a war, one of us must be defeated.

LAURA: Which?

CAPTAIN: The weaker, of course.

LAURA: Does that mean the stronger is in the right?

CAPTAIN: Naturally. Because they have the power.

LAURA: Then I am in the right.

CAPTAIN: Are you so sure you have the power?

LAURA: Yes, the legal power anyway. And tomorrow I shall use it to get you certified. *(long pause)*

CAPTAIN: Certified?

LAURA: Yes, then I shall bring up the child out of the reach of your fantasies.

CAPTAIN: *(after a long pause)* And who will support the child if I am gone.

LAURA: Your pension.

CAPTAIN: *(after a pause)* And how shall you have me certified?

LAURA: *(with letter)* With this letter, a sworn copy of which is already in the hands of the authorities.

CAPTAIN: What letter?

LAURA: Yours. The one in which you admit to your doctor that you have lost your reason.

A blinding light gradually envelops LAURA as she speaks the next lines. THE CAPTAIN watches it grow as if witnessing a vision. LAURA's words reverberate as if they were coming from another sphere, another person.

You have done your job both as a father and a provider. There is no further need for you. So you can go. You realize now that my intelligence is as strong as my will, and since you cannot bear to admit it, you can go.

THE CAPTAIN turns and raises the burning lamp.

*Slowly, he bears down on LAURA, the lamp above
his head. As he hurls it towards her face, there is a
deafening crack of thunder and the stage is consumed
with flames. Simultaneously, BERTHA, THE
NURSE and LAURA appear with flaming torches in
their outstretched hands. They bear down on THE
CAPTAIN, forcing him to the floor. Just before he is
consumed in their fire, the thunderstorm reaches its
most unbearable pitch and the lights snap out.*

*The thunder segues into the sound of frantic
thumping, as of a man trying to pound down a
massive door.*

Lights up.

*Part of the room's furnishings have been removed.
Only the desk and two easy chairs remain.*

LAURA: Did he give you the keys?

NURSE: I took them from his pocket.

LAURA: Give them here.

*Sound of thumping from the up stage door, center-
stage.*

Is that door firmly locked?

NURSE: Yes. My God. My God.

LAURA: Control yourself. We must remain calm.

A knock at the nearby door.

Who's that?

NOJD: *(off-stage)* It's Nojd!

LAURA: Let him in!

THE NURSE rushes out as NOJD dashes in.

NOJD: *(with letter)* It's from the Colonel.

LAURA: Have you emptied the cartridges out of his pistol, as I said?

NOJD: Yes ma'am. Just as you said.

LAURA: Wait outside. I want you to take an answer to the Colonel.

Sound of thumping upstage.

NURSE: What's he doing now?

LAURA: Be quiet. I'm writing!

NURSE: Where will all this end?

LAURA: *(handing her note)* Give this to Nojd — and my mother is not to hear a word about this, do you understand.?

THE NURSE exits as PASTOR enters.

PASTOR: I'm sorry I couldn't get here sooner. It's just incredible.

LAURA: I've never been through a day like it.

PASTOR: At least you're unharmed.

LAURA: But just think what might have happened.

PASTOR: How did it start? I've heard so many conflicting accounts.

LAURA: It started with him raving about not being Bertha's father and ended with him throwing a lighted lamp in my face.

PASTOR: Appalling. He must be quite out of his mind. What's to be done?

LAURA: We must insure there'll be no further outbreaks of violence. The doctor has sent to the hospital for a straitjacket. I've dispatched a message to the Colonel. *(With ledger)* Disgraceful the way he's mismanaged these accounts.

PASTOR: I was afraid something like this might happen. You can't mix fire and water without there being an explosion. *(looks into drawer)* What's all this?

LAURA: This is where he's hidden everything.

PASTOR: *(rummaging)* Good Heavens, it's your old doll and christening cap . . . and Bertha's rattle . . . and your letters. *(beat)* He must have loved you very much to keep all these things.

LAURA: He may have loved me once, but things change.

PASTOR: Laura, tell me. Were you in any way responsible for this?

LAURA: Responsible for a man going mad?

PASTOR: *(pause)* I'll say no more about it. Blood is thicker than water.

LAURA: And what does that mean?

PASTOR: Come, come, This all fits in perfectly with your plan to have complete control of Bertha.

LAURA: I've no idea what you're talking about.

PASTOR: Grisly as it is, I can't help admiring you. And as for me, I suppose I shall be appointed legal guardian to that atheist who I always considered a weed in our garden.

LAURA: *(a short, stifled laugh)* You dare say that to me, his wife?!

PASTOR: How strong you are, Laura. Like a fox in a trap that would sooner bite off its own leg than allow itself to be caught. Like a master thief with no accomplices. No one watches you at work. Not even your own conscience. Look at yourself in the mirror, if you dare.

LAURA: I never use mirrors.

PASTOR: No, you daren't see yourself for what you are. *(takes her hand)* Let's see your hand. Not a speck of blood to betray you. Not a trace of poison. A little innocent murder that the law cannot touch. An unconscious crime. How ingenious.

Sound of thumping.

Listen to him in there. Take care. If that man gets loose, he will saw you in two!

LAURA: You sound as if you're the one with a guilty conscience. Are you accusing me of a crime?

PASTOR: No, I can't do that.

LAURA: Then I am innocent. Now, you look after your charge and I'll look after mine.

THE DOCTOR rushes in.

At last, Doctor. I'm so relieved you've got here although I'm afraid there's not much anyone can do now.

Sound of thumping.

You hear! Are you convinced now?

DOCTOR: I'm convinced there has been an act of violence. The question is whether it was a provoked act of anger or a fit of madness.

PASTOR: Whatever caused it, you must admit his *idee fixe* is . . .

DOCTOR: In one sense, Pastor, your ideas are even more fixed.

PASTOR: My spiritual convictions are in no way comparable to . . .

DOCTOR: Convictions apart, it is now up to you, madame, whether to condemn your husband to imprisonment and a fine, or the asylum. How would you describe the Captain's behavior?

LAURA: I can't say.

DOCTOR: You mean you don't know what would be best for the family? *(beat)* And you, Pastor, what's your view?

PASTOR: It's difficult. There'll be a scandal either way.

LAURA: If he is fined, there may be more violence.

DOCTOR: And if he's sent to prison, he will one day be released. Then it would be best for all parties concerned that he be treated as insane.

THE DOCTOR looks to LAURA who looks to THE PASTOR.

Where is the nurse?

LAURA: Why do you need her?

DOCTOR: She'll be needed to get the patient in the straitjacket after I've had a talk with him. I have it here. Please ask her to come in.

LAURA: *(calling of)* Margaret.

PASTOR: *(avoiding THE DOCTOR's looks)* A dreadful business, dreadful.

THE NURSE enters.

DOCTOR: Now listen carefully. When I give the signal, I want you to approach the Captain from behind and put him into this. Once he's in it, we should be safe from any further outbreaks of violence. You see the sleeves are unusually long to restrict his movements. Fasten these behind his back. These straps go through these buckles here, and can then be tied from behind. *(beat)* Do you think you can do this?

NURSE: No, Doctor, I can't.

LAURA: Why don't you do it yourself?

DOCTOR: Because the patient mistrusts me. You, madam, would be the most appropriate person to do it, but I fear he distrusts you even more. Pastor, perhaps you could . . . ?

PASTOR: No, I'm sorry. Out of the question.

NOJD: *(entering)* I've delivered the letter, madam.

All regard NOJD for a moment.

LAURA: Good. Now, Nojd. You know what's happened. The Captain has had a mental breakdown and we need you to help look after him.

NOJD: If there's anything I can do for the Captain, he knows he can count on me.

DOCTOR: Good. Now take this jacket and . . .

NURSE: *(interceding)* No, he mustn't — he'd hurt him. I'll do it myself. Gently, gently. Let him wait outside. If I need help, I'll call.

Sound of thumping.

DOCTOR: Put this under your shawl . . . everyone else outside. That door won't hold much longer.

Hurry, hurry!

The sound of the thumping behind the upstage door increases.

lights fade to black.

Behind the door, we see a haze of light outlining the cracks in the timber.

The pounding grows to a climax and then the door gives in. As it is shattered into bits, we see the silhouette of THE CAPTAIN in the threshold. He is in his shirtsleeves and holding books under his arms. Slowly he walks out of the upstage light and into the room. THE PASTOR is stage right: THE DOCTOR stage left. When the lights come up again, the desk has disappeared leaving only two easy chairs on the stage.

CAPTAIN: It's all in there y'know; all of it. There's nothing mad about it. For example, The Odyssey, Book 1, line 215. Telemachus to Athene. 'My mother indeed declares that he — meaning Odysseus — is my father; but I myself cannot be sure — since no man knows for certain his own begetter.' And mark now, it was Penelope that was being suspected; that most virtuous of all women. And look here, the prophet Ezekiel: 'The fool saith, "Lo, here is my father, but who can tell from whose loins he hath rightly sprung?" ' That's pretty conclusive, I'd say. What have we got here? History of Russian Literature. 'Alexander Pushkin, one of Russia's greatest poets, died in agony caused more by the rumors of his wife's infidelity than the fatal bullet he received in the chest from a duel. On his deathbed and with his last breath, however, he swore she was innocent.' Jackass! How could he or

anyone swear to something so silly? Oh, I know my
books all right. Don't you worry about that.

Suddenly discovers THE PASTOR.

Ah Jonas, are *you* here? *(turns to DOCTOR)* And
the Doctor, yes, of course. Goes without saying. *(to
PASTOR)* Did I ever tell you what I said to the
English lady who complained that Irishmen threw
lighted lamps into their wive's faces? 'God, what
women,' I said. 'Women,' she simpered. 'Yes,' I
replied, 'When things reach such a pass that a man
who has loved and worshipped a woman, picks up
a lighted lamp and flings it into her face, then you
can be quite certain that . . .'

PASTOR: *(after a pause)* Quite certain that . . .

CAPTAIN: *(suddenly)* That what?

PASTOR: What?

CAPTAIN: Nothing! Nothing at all! One never really
knows anything. One assumes . . . believes . . . is
led to believe . . . that's so, isn't it, Jonas? One
believes, as you'd say, and is saved. But one can
also believe and be lost. Isn't that so?

DOCTOR: Captain . . .

CAPTAIN: *(suddenly hostile)* Be quiet! I don't wish
to hear your voice. You're just a bloody telephone
anyway, aren't you, relaying voices from in there.
Um? Aren't you? Damn right you are! Tell me,
Jonas, I've always meant to ask you this. Do you
believe, since we're on the subject of belief, that
you are the father of your children? Didn't you

used to have a tutor living in your house — a good-
looking chap with beautiful eyes? I remember
there was some talk about all that.

PASTOR: Adolf . . . take care.

CAPTAIN: Just put your hand under your hair there.
Do you feel two little bumps. Good God, he's gone
so pale. Oh, it was just gossip of course, but how
they talked! No stopping them! We're all figures of
fun, Jonas. All of us. Married men! Aren't we,
Doctor? And how firm were the springs on your
marriage bed, eh? Didn't you have some Lieutenant
billeted with you? Just a minute . . . just a
minute . . . wasn't he . . . ? *(approaches THE*
DOCTOR and whispers in his ear) Good God, he's
gone pale as well. No need to fret about that. She's
dead and buried and what's done can't be undone,
can it? By the way, I used to know the chap. I
believe he's now . . . look at me, Doctor . . . no,
straight in the eye . . . a major of Dragoons! *(quickly*
checks Doctor's hair) I'll be damned if he hasn't
sprouted horns as well. It's an epidemic!

DOCTOR: I'd be obliged, Captain, if you changed
the subject.

CAPTAIN: Soon as I mention horns, he wants to change
the subject.

PASTOR: You realize, do you not, Adolf, that you are
not in your right mind?

CAPTAIN: Of course I realize it. But if I had custody
of your horned heads for a week or two, I should
have you shut up, too. I am mad, but how did I
become mad? Is that of any interest to anyone?

(takes photo of BERTHA from breast pocket of shirt) Good God, my daughter. 'My' daughter. Mine. But of course we can never be sure. Do you know what we have to do to prove it conclusively? First, marry in order to be accepted by society. Then divorce immediately. After that, become lovers and finally, adopt the children. Then you can be sure at least, that they're your own adopted children. That's something, isn't it?

Slumps into chair.

But how can all that help me now? How can anything help? Now that my hope of immortality has been taken from me. What good is my science and my philosophy if I've nothing to live for. What good is my life, if I've lost my honor? I took my right arm, half my mind, half my marrow and grafted them onto another stem. I thought they'd grow together there and form a more perfect tree. Then along came someone with a knife and made an incision, just below the graft, so that now I'm only half a tree. The other half keeps on growing with my arm, my mind, my body, while I just wither and die, because it was the best part of me that I gave away Now I want to die. You can do what you like with me. I no longer exist.

THE DOCTOR and PASTOR slowly back away as BERTHA comes forward from upstage towards the slumped figure of THE CAPTAIN who is looking at the photo in his hand.

BERTHA: Are you sick, Father?

CAPTAIN: *(starts, as if the photo has spoken)* Sick?

BERTHA: Do you know what you've done? Thrown a lamp at mother.

CAPTAIN: Did I?

BERTHA: She could have been terribly hurt.

CAPTAIN: Would that matter?

BERTHA: You're not my father if you can say a thing like that.

CAPTAIN: *(looks at her)* Who's told you that? Who is your father then, who?

BERTHA: You couldn't be if you say that.

CAPTAIN: Who then, who? You seem very well informed. That I should live to hear my own child tell me to my face that I'm not her father . . . ? Don't you realize you're insulting your mother by saying that? Don't you see that? If it's true, *she* is disgraced.

BERTHA: I won't have you say anything against mother.

CAPTAIN: Of course not. You're all against me. You've always been.

BERTHA: Father.

CAPTAIN: Don't call me that.

BERTHA: Father, Father, Father!

CAPTAIN: *(trying to avoid her embrace, finally draws*

her to him) Bertha, my baby, my baby. Of course
you're mine. You must be mine. You *are* mine.
Those were just sick thoughts that blew into my
mind like pestilence or fever. Look at me. Look
into my eyes. Let me see my soul in your eyes.
(looks) But I see *her* soul, too. Two souls. You love
me with one and hate me with the other. But you
must only love me. There must be only one soul or
you'll never have peace — nor shall I. You must
have only one mind; child of *my* mind — and one
will, *my* will.

BERTHA: But I don't want that. I want to be myself.

CAPTAIN: I won't allow you that. I'm a cannibal, you
see, and I want to eat you all up. Your mother
wanted to eat me, but she couldn't. I am Saturn
who devoured his children because it was
prophesied that otherwise, they would consume
him. To eat or to be eaten — that is the question.
Unless I eat you, you will eat me. You've already
shown me your teeth. But don't be afraid, my
baby, I shan't do you any harm. Now where is
that . . .? *(turns to pistol, the holster of which is
slung over the chair)*

BERTHA: *(moving away)* Help, help, help!

*BERTHA moves into THE NURSE's arms who
comes on as soon as she hears her cries.*

NURSE: What is it? What is it?

CAPTAIN: Who's taken these cartridges?

NURSE: *(shooing BERTHA away)* I've just tidied
them away, Adolf. Put them into a safe place. Now

sit down and calm yourself and I'll bring them
right back.

*She ushers THE CAPTAIN back into the easy chair
where he remains sitting dully mouthing
indecipherable words. The straightjacket is wrapped
in her shawl behind the chair.*

Do you remember, Adolf, when you were my little
baby and I used to tuck you up at night and read
you the Bible. And do you remember how I used
to get up in the night and bring you a drink, and
how I used to light the candle by your bed and tell
you little stories when you had bad dreams and
couldn't sleep. Do you remember?

CAPTAIN: Keep talking, Margaret. It soothes me to
hear you. Go on . . . go on.

NURSE: And do you remember that time you took
the big carving knife to make boats with, and you
wouldn't give it back until I'd told you a story. You
were such a stubborn little baby, we had to play
little tricks on you because you wouldn't believe
we knew what was best for you. 'Now give me that
little snake, I said — or he'll bite you with his
sharp, little teeth.' And you'd let go of the knife.
*(takes pistol from hand and places it on floor behind
chair)* And all those times you wouldn't get your
clothes on and we had to coax you, and I'd promise
to give you a lovely gold coat, just like a prince
wears. And then I'd take your little woolen jacket
and say, 'In with your arms now. All in one go!
That's right!'.

*She pauses, holding the arms of the straitjacket out
in front of THE CAPTAIN who is reliving the scene*

*being described. After a painfully long pause, he
shoves his arms into the outstretched garment.*

Then I'd say, 'Now sit nice and still while I button
it down the back' and 'Oh, you're dressed so lovely
now. Just like a little prince in a gold coat.' And
then I'd say, 'Now get up, like a good little boy,
and walk across the room so we can see how nice it
fits.' *(after a pause, THE CAPTAIN rises and as the
child he was, shambles slowly across the room)* And
then I'd say, 'Now it's time to go to bed'.

CAPTAIN: Go to bed? When I've just got dressed?
That would be a . . . *(stops. The childish memory
begins to vanish. Jerks his arms. Realizes he cannot
move. Slowly coming out of his dream, looks down
to discover the straitjacket. Then quietly)* What have
you done to me? Fiend! Witch! Who would have
thought you had the cunning. Bound, fleeced,
cozened! Why can't I just be allowed to die.

NURSE: Forgive me, Adolf, I couldn't let you kill the
child.

CAPTAIN: Why not? Life is hell and it's death that
brings the Kingdom of Heaven and that's where
children belong.

NURSE: What do you know about hereafter?

CAPTAIN: That's all one does know about. About
life, one knows nothing at all. If one only realized
that at the start.

NURSE: Humble your heart, Adolf, and pray to God
for mercy. — It's not too late even now. It wasn't
too late for the thief on the Cross when the Savior
said 'Today shalt thou be with me in Paradise.'

CAPTAIN: Croaking over my corpse already, you old crow. Nojd! Nojd!

NOJD enters hurriedly.

Throw this wretch out of here. She'll suffocate me with her blasted hymn books. Throw her out the window — or up the chimney — anywhere you like, but out of here!

NOJD: God help me, Captain, I can't do that. I'd take on half-a-dozen men if you like, but I can't lay hands on a woman.

CAPTAIN: See how they've laid hands on me?

NOJD: I can't, Captain. It's like striking the Pastor. It's like religion. It's in your blood. I just can't.

LAURA enters and gestures NOJD out. THE CAPTAIN fixes his eyes on her.

CAPTAIN: Omphale, Omphale. Play with your club while Hercules spins your wool.

LAURA: Am I your enemy, Adolf?

CAPTAIN: You're all my enemies. My mother, who didn't want to bring me into the world because it would bring her pain, was my enemy. She drained my embryo of its nourishment, so that I was almost deformed. My sister, who trained me to serve her like a vassal, she was my enemy. The first woman I held in my arms was my enemy. She gave me ten years of disease in return for the love I gave her. My daughter became my enemy, having to choose between me and you. And you, my wife, you have always been my mortal enemy. You wouldn't rest until you'd squeezed the life out of me.

LAURA: I never planned nor intended what has happened. I may have had a vague desire to be rid of you because you stood between me and my child, but there was never a conscious plan behind r.1y actions. I just slid onto the rails which you had laid down, but as God is my judge, I swear I am innocent even if I am not. You were like a stone on my heart, pressing down harder and harder, until I could no longer bear the weight of it. If I have brought you to this, it was not intentional and I ask your forgiveness.

CAPTAIN: That sounds plausible — even to me, but what good is it? Fault? Who can find the fault? Perhaps the whole notion of marriage is the fault. Once upon a time, a man took a wife to his bosom, now he enters into a partnership with a woman or sets up house with a friend. And then he violates the partner and debauches the friend. Whatever happened to love? Healthy, sensual love? It died somewhere along the way, of neglect I suppose. And what happens to the shares of that love, payable to holder, drawn on an account that's entirely bunkrupt? Who can honor those shares when the crash comes? Who is the tangible father to the spiritual child?

LAURA: Your suspicions about the child are completely unfounded.

CAPTAIN: Even that is horrible. If they were real, at least there'd be something to grasp hold of, to cling to. Now there are only shadows, lurking in the undergrowth, peering out at me with lewd, grinning faces. It's like fighting windmills. A mock battle

with blank cartridges. If I'd really been betrayed,
I'd have stirred my mind and body to action — but
now, my thoughts just disintegrate. My brain
grinds at emptiness until it catches fire. Give me a
pillow, for pity's sake. Put something over me. I'm
so cold; so cold.

*LAURA spreads her shawl over him while THE
NURSE draws the second easy chair over, making a
makeshift bed of the two. THE CAPTAIN's legs are
placed onto the second chair. LAURA tucks the
shawl around him.*

(looking up tenderly) I would give you my hand,
but it's tied behind my back. Omphale! Omphale!
I can feel your soft wool against my lips. It's warm
and gentle and smells of vanilla like your hair used
to when you were a girl and we used to walk
together among the birches. There was primrose
then, and thrushes. Oh it was beautiful, beautiful.
How beautiful life was then, and now . . . it's
turned to this. You didn't want it and I didn't want
it and yet it's happened. Who guides the motions
of our lives?

LAURA: God.

CAPTAIN: *(sarcastic)* Mars, more likely. The God of
War. Or the Goddess. Who's put this cat over me?
Take it away. Away I say. And bring me my uniform.
Put my tunic over me.

*LAURA's shawl is removed and THE NURSE
drapes THE CAPTAIN's military tunic over him.*

My rough lion-skin that they tried to take from me.
Omphale! Omphale! Such cunning! She so loved
peace she invented the art of disarming men. Wake
up, Hercules! They're stealing away your club!

You'd turn our shining armor into tinsel. But before it was tinsel, it *was* iron. Iron! In the old days, it was the smith with his hammer who forged the soldier's coat of mail. Now it's the seamstress with her needle. Omphale, Omphale. Bold strength vanquished by subtle cunning. Curse you, you and your whole sex. *(spits at LAURA)* What kind of pillow is this. It's hard and cold. Margaret, come and sit beside me.

MARGARET does so.

Let me put my head against you. Warm. Cosy. Bend over me so I can feel your breast. Oh, it's so good to sleep on a woman's breast — a mother's or a mistress's — although a mother's is best.

LAURA: Adolf . . . do you want to see your child?

CAPTAIN: A man has no children. Only women have children. We always die childless. 'Gentle Jesus, meek and mild, look upon a little child . . .'

NURSE: Listen. He's praying to God.

CAPTAIN: *(eyes opening)* No. To you. Put me to sleep. I'm so drowsy. Good night, sweet Margaret, blessed among women . . .

He raises himself as if to kiss THE NURSE, strains there for a moment then falls back into the chair.

As he does so, the lights pull down to a small pool around him. THE DOCTOR and PASTOR have entered. THE DOCTOR rushes to THE CAPTAIN and begins taking his pulse.

DOCTOR: He's had a stroke.

PASTOR: Is he gone?

DOCTOR: No. He might regain consciousness, but in what state, I dread to think.

PASTOR: 'First death, and then judgement . . .,

DOCTOR: It's not for us to judge or to accuse. You who believe there is a God that rules over human destiny, must plead his cause to heaven.

NURSE: With his last breath, he prayed to God.

PASTOR: Is it true? (looking to LAURA who remains non-committal).

DOCTOR: My skill is useless. You must try yours now, Pastor.

LAURA: Is that all you can say at his death bed?

DOCTOR: I can do no more. Let him who knows more, speak.

BERTHA enters, sees THE CAPTAIN prostrate in the two chairs, begins to move towards him. LAURA takes her by the shoulder then with one arm around BERTHA and the other around THE NURSE, slowly moves back from the dead CAPTAIN, the praying PASTOR and the mourning DOCTOR.

After a moment, the men become aware of the three women huddled together at some distance from themselves. Slowly, they turn towards them. As they do so, the three women, unified by an inexplicable solidarity, raise their heads and look defiantly at the men before them.

Fade out to black.

Curtain.